T0099168

The Angels' Book
of Promises

The Angels' Book of Promises

Billy Roberts

6th BOOKS

Winchester, UK
Washington, USA

First published by Sixth Books, 2012
Sixth Books is an imprint of John Hunt Publishing Ltd., Laurel House, Station Approach,
Alresford, Hants, SO24 9JH, UK
office1@jhpbooks.net
www.johnhuntpublishing.com
www.6th-books.com

For distributor details and how to order please visit the 'Ordering' section on our website.

Text copyright: Billy Roberts 2011

ISBN: 978 1 78099 162 7

All rights reserved. Except for brief quotations in critical articles or reviews, no part of this
book may be reproduced in any manner without prior written permission from the publishers.

The rights of Billy Roberts as author have been asserted in accordance with the Copyright,
Designs and Patents Act 1988.

A CIP catalogue record for this book is available from the British Library.

Design: Lee Nash

Printed and bound by CPI Group (UK) Ltd, Croydon, CR0 4YY
Printed in the USA by Offset Paperback Mfrs, Inc

We operate a distinctive and ethical publishing philosophy in all
areas of our business, from our global network of authors to
production and worldwide distribution.

CONTENTS

INTRODUCTION

It is said that mediums are born and not made, and also that a medium's life will never be easy. I was born on June 24th 1946 in Wavertree a suburb of Liverpool, in the north of England, at a time when the country was still recovering from the pounding it had received from the German bombers during the so-called Blitz of the Second World War. My mother, her sister and their mother were all mediums, and although my father did not have any interest at all in things of a spiritual nature, he apparently accepted it all as being an integral part of my mother's life. When I was born, my parents, Annie and Albert Roberts already had a ten year old son also called Albert, or Alby as he was more affectionately known, and so as far as my father was concerned his family was now complete. The morning of the day my mother went into labour with me she found a very old and bent crucifix on the step and took this to be some sort of omen regarding the child to which she was about to give birth. Her assumption was correct and my life was to be extremely difficult, in more ways than one.

From a very early age I had become acquainted with Tall Pine or TP as he is still affectionately known, my disembodied guardian and spiritual mentor. Tall Pine is a spirit guide and someone who is as close to me today as he was when I first became aware of him. As a child Tall Pine was a frequent visitor, and I would always see his extremely tall figure in the corner of my bedroom, watching me from the shadows.

From as far back as my first year on this planet I had become well and truly accustomed to my angelic visitors, although at that young age I had no idea what they were. All that I knew was that they were different to Tall Pine in both appearance and the feelings they brought to me. Their visits became a regular occurrence, and although my mother told me in later years that she too saw them with me on many occasions, at that time she had no idea that they were most probably a warning of the life that lay ahead of me. At the age of three I developed an incurable respiratory disease called Bronchiectasis, necessitating long periods in Alder Hey Children's Hospital, Liverpool, England. Because the treatment for such a disease was quite primitive in the late 1940s, in comparison to what it is today, the prognosis was bleak; my parents were told in no uncertain terms that I would most probably not live to see my tenth birthday. As a consequence of this I was mollycoddled and given everything I wanted. During long bouts of illness I would be visited by beings in gowns of shimmering light. I became extremely accustomed to them as their visits became more and more frequent, regardless of whether I was laid-up at home, or lying in a hospital bed.

My first significant angel encounter took place whilst I was recovering from a bout of pneumonia at home. I was upstairs alone when the room was suddenly filled with intense white light much brighter than the afternoon sun flooding through the window. A sweet fragrance accompanied the visitation and I was overwhelmed with a sense of peace and calm. Two figures I had never seen before stood at the end of my bed resplendent in shimmering gowns of light, and although no words fell from their lips, I just knew what they were thinking. They told me that their names were Mela and Aema and that they were always going to watch over and guide me through my life and beyond and that they would come whenever I needed them. For a three year old child this was all too easy and calling them almost became a game that frequently helped me pass the time away.

It is also so easy to cynically dismiss my anecdotal accounts of angels as no more than the wild imaginings of a sickly child; but the truth is that the memories I have today of my childhood encounters with angels have never faded and are as vivid and clear today as they were the very first time I saw them. Even if you do cynically dismiss angels as being no more than farfetched and fanciful, born out of the wishful thinking of the weak and the poor, they have nonetheless always been there relentless in every culture and throughout every age. It is true that those who believe in angels do have their own ideas of what they look like, and those who simply accept them as integral parts of their own religion see them as the archetypal beings with which they have been brought up, statuesque figures with powerful wings. If, like me, you just *know* that angels exist, then you won't have any difficulty at all understanding what I have written, and exactly why I have written it.

I began creating my first Angels Book of Promises sometime around the age of five, primarily at first as a means of expressing my feelings about my life in general. I began to write down the things I desperately wanted, just in the way a child writes a letter to Santa Claus; but I was asking the angels looking after me for something more than just presents. In my child-like way I soon realised that I had created a fool-proof and very reliable and effective way of calling the angels to me whenever I needed their help. It soon became quite apparent to me that Mela and Aema were not the only ones I could contact; my Angels' Book of Promises somehow opened a door to a whole new world for me. My Angels' Book of Promises was a way of transcending prayer and eventually became an extremely effective 'bargaining tool' that worked primarily on the age-old precepts, 'Fair exchange is no robbery!' Or, 'One good turn deserves another.' To the devoutly religious person this might sound a little disrespectful, but I had discovered an ideal way of reaching out to someone other than my mother, and my Angels' Book of Promises was also an effective way of working out my many problems and at least sharing them with someone not of this world. Although I didn't realise it I had unknowingly created a psychological tool that was extremely therapeutic for me.

And so, although my communications with angels were originally born from the fact that I was a sickly child with a bleak future, over the years my relationship with these Celestial beings has grown into something else and has become far more meaningful and much more profound.

Whilst my early childhood was quite daunting, and much of it was spent in hospital away from my family, my life really became more traumatic when I started infant school. I was not one for rough and tumble games, and so I always seemed to be on the edge of the playground sadly looking in at the other children playing. As a result of this I was sent to what was then called an 'Open-Air' school for frail children. There I was amongst other children who did not feel a need to compete, climb trees or fight each other. As far as my parents were concerned Underlea, as it was called, was the ideal environment for their sickly little boy.

SEEING DEAD PEOPLE

Although seeing so-called 'dead' people was commonplace to me, (just like the boy in the movie Sixth Sense) it never occurred to me for one moment that other children were not the same. Little did I know that I was being observed by the school nurse, who quickly became concerned about my psychological well-being. She suggested that because of my unusual behaviour and the things I was saying to teachers and the other children, I should be assessed by a child psychologist, just to make certain there was no underlying psychological problem. I could hear the voices of so-called 'dead' people as well as actually see them, and this in itself gave the school authorities some cause for concern. My parents reluctantly agreed for me to see a psychologist, and on the conclusion of my two hour consultation, the gently spoken lady psychologist diagnosed that primarily because of my illness and frequent stays in hospital, I was extremely sensitive and insecure, and also that I was creative and possessed a vivid imagination. She was correct on all counts. However, her prognosis that I would eventually grow out of it was not. My psychic skills persisted and my disembodied encounters continued.

THE LADY OF LIGHT

It was about then that I had my second very poignant angel experience, and the one that seemed to touch everyone in our family, including my father, even though he did not actually see it. I was playing *ghosts* in the front room of our house, and trying desperately to frighten my friend, Tommy Edgar, by turning the light on and off and making ghostly wailing sounds. Tommy asked me to stop messing around and turn the light back on. To my great surprise this time it wouldn't go back on. My first thought was that I'd done something to the light and that my father would come into the room at any moment to shout at me. I tried to open the door to check the other lights were on, when suddenly there was a loud popping sound followed by a bright light glowing on the wall above an old cabinet that my father had purchased in an auction sale some weeks before. My friend and I stood there speechless, just watching the bright light amazed as it slowly expanded into the room before metamorphosing into the shape of a beautiful lady draped in long robes. As we watched the apparition, it grew in intensity and size and then gradually became a three-dimensional image, with clearly defined features. At that point my friend became very distressed and ran to the door, pulling frantically at the handle until the door swung open, allowing him to make a hasty retreat. I thought all the commotion would cause my mother to investigate, but they seemed to be oblivious to what was going on in the adjacent room. I had always been very religious and was transfixed by my ethereal visitor. By now the lady of light (as I called her) was as real and tangible as any living person, and was smiling at me with outstretched arms. Something made me run quickly from the room to fetch my mother. 'Our Lady is here!' I called. 'Come quickly!' My father was relaxing with his feet up on a stool and refused to move, but my mother and Aunt Sadie followed me into the parlour as we called it. Looking back now I am certain that they did not expect to see what they did as both were speechless and stood there dumbfounded as they looked upon the lady surrounded in a beautiful light, her gown shimmering through the darkened room. My mother mumbled something to Aunt Sadie and then suggested that perhaps the lady of light had come to make me better. She led me over to the apparition and told me to reach out and touch her gown. However, before my hand made contact with the Lady of Light, the same popping sound that had brought her there in the first place caused the light to go on in the room and the lady to disappear completely. Upon closer inspection my mother found a film of iridescent pink powder across the surface of the cabinet and spread across the floor where the apparition had been. She collected this into an empty pill bottle for a keepsake, and looking quite bewildered by the whole experience, they both went back into the living room to tell my father. I must say, although he had initially appeared disinterested now he too looked somewhat shocked by what he had been told.

The following day a neighbour my mother had told about the apparition called with three nuns who wanted to pray at the spot where, as they believed, Our Lady had appeared. They asked to see the iridescent pink powder, but when my mother opened the pill bottle it was completely empty. Although everyone was mystified by the whole ghostly experience, the Lady of Light's appearance preceded a sequence of tragic and very unhappy experiences in our family. I was taken into hospital a week later with lobar pneumonia and my mother became very ill with a thyroid condition and had to be hospitalised for a short while. To add to all that, my father was badly burned when a can of petrol ignited after someone had lit a cigarette as he was refuelling his van. Although he was badly burned, he was very lucky to be alive! The nuns later suggested that the apparition in the front room was to reassure us that we would survive all the turbulence and heartache, which of course we did. It made me totally aware that from a very young age I was without any doubt living my life Beneath the Wings of Angels, and so it still is today.

Although my parents had been warned many times that they should not expect me to live, I just knew that the consultant's dismal prognosis was wrong.

As a child it always seemed as though I was living my life in two very different worlds, and those who visited me from the 'other' world were as tangible to me as everybody else. My angel encounters continued and I defied the cold predictions of the hospital consultants and survived. At the age of thirteen I showed an aptitude for the guitar, and when I left school in 1962 at the age of 16, I was already living the dream of every other kid my age, playing lead guitar in a rock band and touring Europe with some of the biggest names in the world of music. By 1965 at the age of 19 I was living between Paris and Brussels, supporting such musical giants as Chuck Berry, Jimi Hendrix, The Kinks, The Moody Blues, American blues veteran, Memphis Slim, to mention but a few. During that period of my life although I was always very much aware that I was still living beneath the wings of angels, I never actually used my Angels' Book of Promises as a means of communicating with them. Little wonder then that I gradually lost my way and allowed my life to slowly spiral out of control when I found myself pulled into the dismal world of narcotics. I was in and out of rehabilitation units for 12 months in a feeble attempt to cure me of my addiction. However, I seemed to be fighting a losing battle, and at the beginning of 1970 I became very ill and returned to the UK to be cared for by my mother. From that point everything seemed to go wrong when the cold hand of fate intervened and my father died after a short illness with pancreatic cancer. My world had fallen apart and I really found it extremely difficult to continue living. It was at the lowest point in my life that my angelic friends came back with a vengeance, making it abundantly clear to me that my music career was over, and that I now had to follow a completely different vocation as a medium. I know this may sound quite far-fetched to a sceptic, but I am now far too long in the tooth to care what others think. Making a career as a medium had never been a practical option; nor was it something I had ever contemplated doing. However, it now looked as though my fate was in the hands of God, and I now began to realise that this was most probably the very reason I had contracted a life-threatening illness as a child.

BEGINNING LIFE ALL OVER AGAIN

During my period of recovery from drug addiction I looked at my childhood Angels' Book of Promises and decided to create a new updated version of it. This was a unique and effective way of reaffirming my relationship with the angels, particularly those responsible for specific tasks. It really did amaze me just how quick and effective the book actually was. It was so simple. I did exactly as I did as a child and created the perfect Angels' Book of Promises. It was unbelievably so simple – so simple that a child could do it. In fact, a child did do it – me!

In my adult life the Angels' Book of Promises also served as a psychological exercise and discipline and helped me to focus my consciousness on an external source that transcended the parameters of the physical universe. This may sound very metaphysical but it was exactly what I needed at that time. The more I worked at re-affirming my relationship with the angels the more methods I was inspired to create. And so I was able to formulate a complete programme of angel techniques that complemented my Angels' Book of Promises and enabled me to have a much deeper understanding of angels, the Universe and the Laws of Attraction. This programme involved Angel Meditations, primarily to help with my attunement; Angel scrying techniques that helped me to focus more efficiently; special Angel Prayers that helped to strengthen as well as deepen my relationship with them; also Angel finger movements, based on the Hindu and Buddhist Mudras, to be used primarily as marks of respect, just as you would put your hands together in prayer. All these combined with my Angels' Book of Promises allowed me to access higher states of consciousness, and enabled me to have a much deeper understanding of Angels and the Celestial Light. It has always worked for me and there's no reason at all why it cannot work for you in the fulfilment of your dreams, your aspirations, your endeavours and your prayers. The Angels' Book of Promises is your own personal way of establishing a relationship with angels. It should never be touched by anyone but you, and it is empowered by your faith and belief that it will work. Although a simple book, it should always be cared for and treated as you would treat any holy book – with great respect.

They do say that hindsight is a wonderful thing; however, when I now look back on my life I can see it with much more clarity, and now fully understand the Universal law of Attraction. Cynics and religious bigots have frequently criticised my past involvement with drugs, with the crass comment that I could not have made such a radical transformation, and that surely angels would be more interested in someone who has led an exemplary life. A man is who he is today as result of whom he was yesterday. I know beyond a shadow of doubt that I am only alive today because I was helped by angels. If some people find that offensive that is their problem and certainly not mine.

CALLING TO ANGELS

They do say that in times of great sorrow and need the cries of the soul resound through the universe, until it creates a kindred impulse with one, or even more angelic beings. Prayer most certainly makes a 'connection' with angels, as do certain methods of meditation. But when the angels come where exactly do they come from? There have been suggestions that angels are terrestrial beings from a far off universe – even from a far off time, and that we humans are constantly being observed, almost as though the human race as a whole is taking part in some great cosmic experiment. Medieval artists always depicted angels with powerful feathered wings, enabling them to descend from heaven. There is now very little doubt that the idea of wings was only created in the first place to explain how an angel could traverse between heaven and earth; but in reality angels possess the power to move unseen between our world and the next in the blinking of an eye. We must then pose the question: 'Why should angels choose to help us in our hour of need? And, what is in it for them?' I am quite certain that by helping us they also help themselves to evolve spiritually or perhaps even to rise to much higher worlds. Although as a child I prayed every night before I climbed into bed, I couldn't help but ask why we had to pray at all when God should be able to see exactly what is in our hearts and minds even before the words are brought to our lips. Today I look upon prayer as the externalisation of my thoughts as they are released into the universe as an incredible affirmation. I still pray; in fact, I need to pray, and not just before I climb into bed either, but every time I have a few moments to spare. I am quite sure that prayer is a great mental release, and something that must be learned.

There is definitely a technique to the art of praying, and some people find it extremely difficult. Prayer must not be chanted mechanically, without thinking about what you are saying. Prayer is an extremely effective way of placing your thoughts in some semblance of order, before releasing them into the atmosphere, with an even great force than the one with which they were first created. As a child I saw the universe as an incredible *Listening device* that enabled angelic beings to Tune-in to our prayers. I have never thought for one moment that our prayers are ever wasted, even when they appear not to be answered. By praying on a regular basis we are creating a suitable atmosphere in which to live in the future, both for ourselves and for the planet as a whole. We are constantly peopling our own private portion of space by the way we think. Working then on this premise we are most certainly the architects of our own destinies, not only by the way we think, but also by the way our thoughts are reflected in the life that we live. Buddha said: *'You don't get what you want, you get who you are!'* That explains perfectly the process of thought and the way in which our life is affected by the way we think. The mind is the common denominator; it can heal and it can destroy. If, as the saying goes, *'you can think your way into an early grave,'* then through the same process, you can most certainly think your way into a healthier, happier and wealthier life. You may say, 'What has all this got to do with angels and the Angels' Book of Promises?' Well, it has got a lot to do with angels and the way we attract them into our lives by the way we think and also by the way we dream. You can tell a man's true worth by the angels that watch over him. How true that is! You can also tell the quality of a man's mind by the shadow it casts! The quality of our life is without a doubt a reflection of the way we think, and the way we think is the way we are. We must always keep evil in sight, but never walk in its shadow. Following this precept empowers the soul and helps to re-affirm one's allegiance to God and the kingdom of angels.

Although I have now been a professional medium for just over thirty years, I have conducted lectures, workshops and seminars all over the world, and have been astounded by the amount of people who are truly interested and believe in the existence of angels. Early in my career as a medium I made certain not to talk about my experiences or voice my feelings and opinions about these *Ambassadors of Light,* as I have now come to know them. However, today because of the growing interest in angels I now feel more comfortable in sharing with you my thoughts and experiences in this book, *THE ANGELS' BOOK OF PROMISES.*

The Angels' Book of Promises is a psychological and spiritual discipline culminating into an easy to follow instruction manual on how to establish a relationship with angels and to call them whenever you need *their* help. My methods are completely original and have always worked for me. I find them as effective now as I did when I was a young boy, and I do know that they WILL work as efficiently for you. The Angels' Book of Promises will not only help you to evoke sacred forces, but it will also help you to establish your place in the Universe of Angels.

In my younger years working as a professional medium was never an option; however, I do now believe that I had to go through all that I did in preparation for the work I do today. I frequently feel that my mediumistic abilities were imposed upon me against my will, and that I was given a cross that at times I can scarcely bear. In the past I have tried on numerous occasions to re-visit my profession as a musician, only to find that something always happens to bring me once again to my knees. I have long since accepted that I have a vocation to follow and not a job of work to do, and that my Angelic visitors have always been there to guide and watch over every step I have taken. Of course there will be some who will dismiss this book as being far-fetched, but as long as it brings about a greater realisation of angels and helps those who desperately need to be helped then I can take all the adverse criticism that is thrown at me. I am not known as a radical medium for nothing!

BILLY ROBERTS

CHAPTER ONE

WHO AND WHAT ARE ANGELS?

I suppose it is all so easy to dismiss the anecdotal accounts of others with disdain and cynicism, and I know that the subject of angels is one that the majority of people do not take too seriously. But the truth is more people than we know have had some form of angelic encounter without even realising it; for an experience with angels can present simply as an unusual moment; a chance meeting with someone who offers you some kind words; a shaft of light streaming through the window on a dismal day, or even a sweet fragrance that causes memories of those long since gone to flood your mind. Angels do not always appear in person, but when they do you can rest assured that the experience will change your life forever.

The Greek word for Angel is *Angelos*, meaning 'messenger'; in Hebrew it is *Malakh*, meaning Divine Spirit or messenger. In Persian Angel is *Angeros*, meaning 'Courier', in Indian culture it is *Garudas*, and in the Koran angel is Malaikah, again meaning messenger. However, it is the general consensus of opinion in all cultures that Angels are messengers of God whose duty is to serve mankind.

My own interest in angels began from that very early age. I realised that in times of distress and heartache it is possible to call upon angelic beings for help. Just as a devout Catholic will pray to a particular saint for help, it is possible for you to pray to the angel watching over you for support, encouragement and to deliver you from the turbulence of an unhappy life. I learned that Archangels were beings of a different kind and far more superior. Unlike the ordinary angel Archangels see to the needs of groups of people and even nations as opposed to single individuals. An Angel is thought to be an intermediate between God and Man. Jews, Zoroastrians, Christians and Muslims believe in Angels. A 14th century work on the celestial hierarchy named nine orders or choirs of Angels with Seraphim in the first rank and Cherubim in the second. Angel Gabriel is represented as having the special duty of revealing God's *will* to man. Many of our ideas about Angels have in fact come from Milton and Dante. In Christian religious tradition Gabriel is one of the seven archangels. In Hebrew Gabriel means 'God is my strong one'. In the Book of Daniel Gabriel brings to the prophet the interpretation of his vision. In the Gospel of Luke he announces to Zacharias the birth of John the Baptist, and to Mary the birth of Christ. Christian tradition represents Gabriel blowing the trumpet on the day of resurrection. In post-biblical Jewish literature, Gabriel sometimes appears as the Angel of Death. In the Talmud he is represented as presiding over thunderstorms. The Koran teaches that Gabriel, Michael, Uriel and Raphael were the four Angels whom God most preferred, and that it was Gabriel who dictated the Koran to Mohammed, 'with the sound of bells.' Raphael is regarded as the 'healing' angel, and many nurses and doctors claim to be guided in their work by him.

They watch over struggling nations in times of strife, famine and war. In Judaism and Christianity the most important of these are the seven Archangels, Gabriel, Michael, Raphael, Uriel, Joophiel, Zadkiel, and the fallen Archangel, Samuel (Samael) or Satan. Uriel is also regarded as the angel of death and is frequently seen at the bedsides of the dying, to help their transition into the other world. Michael is also believed to be the 'Warrior Angel' leading armies into battle and giving strength to soldiers in times of need. One of the lesser known angels is Metratron, considered to be one of the highest angels in the Merkabah and Kabbalist mysticism. Although generally speaking the Archangels do not answer when called upon by individuals in distress, they do instruct those angels on a lower vibratory level to respond to the prayerful call. Samuel, however, is different; he is able to infiltrate the lives of all those whose intentions are not honourable, good or holy. When calling upon the angelic kingdom for help, it is vitally important that your intentions are sincere and unselfish. Although angelic beings are always ready and willing to help even the dishonest of the human race (as long as there is a sincere desire to change), should there be an ulterior motive when calling upon them one must be prepared to take the consequences, as there are also angels whose job it is to supervise the law of cause and effect; or, Karma, as it is known in Eastern traditions.

Although many people pray to certain angels for help in their lives, once you have fully empowered your Angels' Book of Promises its use will transcend prayer and help Angelic forces to know exactly who you are and what you are about.

It is not exactly certain where the concept of angels, winged celestial beings originated, but what is known is that from time immemorial man has held on firmly to the belief that such beings do exist, ambassadors of a Supreme Omnipotent power, that come to his rescue in times of great need. Needless to say, my angelic visitors rarely had wings, and when they did they did not consist of white feathers, but powerful shafts of golden light. Although a minority of those who have actually seen angels have described them as having powerful feathered wings on their back, the majority say that they simply had powerful shafts of light and brought with them overwhelming feelings of peace and serenity. It is now quite clear that the idea of angels having powerful wings was really to explain how these beings could descend from heaven; when in reality Angels can traverse between heaven and earth, unseen and in the blinking of an eye.

ANGELS WITNESSED BY THOUSANDS OF PEOPLE

Psychotherapist, Dr Susan Blackmore, believes that angel sightings are merely apparitions created by the brain in times of crisis to provide comfort. But if this is the case why have so many people actually had an encounter with Angelic beings. A prime example is the Angel of the River Thames, witnessed by thousands of people for centuries.

From as far back as the Great Plague in Britain in 1665 hundreds of sightings of the so-called Angel of the Thames have been reported by ordinary people. The Bubonic plague, carried by rat fleas, ravaged Britain, taking the lives of many thousands of people. With London's trade links the disease was very difficult to contain and quickly spread from one town to another. The so-called Angel of the Thames was an apparition of an angelic being of light, seemingly with wings, that appeared to hundreds of people, who believed that the phenomenon was some sort of a 'sign' from God to reassure the people of London that their plight was nearing an end. Ironically, the plague was completely eradicated when London was yet again brought to its knees in 1666, this time by a great fire that broke out in a bakery in Pudding Lane which then ravaged through its streets and timber houses for five days, destroying three quarters of the city, but miraculously only killing six people. The rats that carried the plague were effectively all destroyed by the fire, putting an end once and for all to the Black Death. The six people killed in the Great Fire of London were buried at what is now known as Jubilee Gardens in a service attended by King Charles11, whom it is said, personally carried buckets of water to help extinguish the raging inferno. Because the Angel once made an appearance at Jubilee Gardens many believed that it represented the spirits of the six people who were killed in the Great Fire.

News of the Angel of the Thames quickly spread from one town to another attracting many people to the River Thames in the hope of catching a glimpse of the Angel many saw as a 'saviour' sent from God. And so the story of the Angel of the Thames grew into an urban legend, mixing fact with fiction, and making some of the anecdotal evidence into something the apparition was not. Over the following weeks, those working on the rebuilding of London reported 'Holy Apparitions' in the ruins around the Thames. There were six sightings of the Angel at this point over the Thames, one of which was even witnessed by the famous diarist, Samuel Pepys. The Angel was looked upon as a good omen to reassure the people of London that the grief of the plague and the Great Fire was now over. Although there were no further sightings of the Angel of the Thames during 1666, over the following years the angel's appearances were fairly consistent. There were Angelic appearances over the River Thames during both the First and Second World Wars, when the apparitions were actually caught on film. In 1951, the year of the Festival of Britain and even later, the Thames Angel appeared simultaneously in two different places. As well as being witnessed by hundreds of people, these occurrences were also caught on film. Many experts believe that the Angelic apparition appeared primarily because London is one of the biggest cities in the world and was nearly completely destroyed by the plague and the Great Fire.

In 1865 dozens of workmen excavating the Thames embankment witnessed the Angelic Apparition, and after there were sightings of the Angel over the Tower of London.

At the outbreak of the 1914 war, many people turned up at Southwark Docks after there had been innumerable reports of the sighting of the Angel of the Thames, no doubt a grim warning of the war that was to come. Again just before the end of the 1914 - 1918 war the apparition of the Angel appeared clearly in front of Cleopatra's Needle, some believe as a symbol of triumph and to portend peace. More currently the Angel of the Thames has been witnessed by hundreds of people at Waterloo Bridge, and with the sophisticated photographic equipment available today, there are many photographs and video footage to confirm the sightings. The apparition is believed to be the manifestation of an Archangel, a celestial being who takes care of nations, unlike an ordinary angel who is believed to look after individual people.

The Thames Angel is still witnessed by hundreds of tourists today, and so I think we can safely dismiss the psychological or optical phenomenon Apophenia, seeing things in random images.

People from all over the world, with many different religious beliefs, have claimed to have been helped by a celestial being of light in times of despair and great need. North Carolina housewife and mother, Coleen Banton's handicapped daughter, Chelsea was put on a ventilator when she was in a critical condition with pneumonia. She was not responding to treatment and doctors had warned her mother to expect the worst. Reluctantly she gave the medical team caring for Chelsea permission to turn off the life-support, and just waited helplessly at her daughter's bedside for her to die. Coleen left the room for a moment to have a quiet word with one of the nurses caring for her daughter. Whilst they were both in the corridor, engrossed in conversation, they saw an intense white light, so bright that they could scarcely look at it. Coleen and the nurse watched in amazement as the unusual light anomaly slowly metamorphosed into the shape of an angel glowing brightly. It remained there for no longer than five minutes, during which time Coleen was able to take a photograph of it with her phone. At that point one of the doctors excitedly called Coleen back into the room. They were astounded to see that Chelsea was now breathing without the aid of a ventilator, and was even showing signs of recovery. Although the medical team were astounded, Coleen was certain her daughter's recovery had something to do with the appearance of the angel in the corridor. Although her daughter is still handicapped, she did make a complete recovery from the respiratory condition that very nearly took her life, and today she lives quite happily with her family. Coleen now lives her life with the full and certain knowledge that they do have their own very special

Guardian Angel watching over them. Chelsea's story was shown on television in 2010 in a programme that highlighted people's experiences with angels.

Many who claim to have had an encounter with an angel have said that the experience left them with an overwhelming feeling of peace and happiness. Those who have witnessed an apparition of an angel have stated that the actual visitation was accompanied by a sweet fragrance that clung to the air. Interestingly enough, the majority of those who have seen angels have said that the celestial figure they saw did not have powerful white wings, as depicted in medieval paintings, but simply appeared as an ordinary person dressed in a shimmering white gown with intense white light exuding from them. One particular angel visitation took place in a small church in a quaint village in Herefordshire, England, during the Christening of a young woman before she could marry her partner of 6 years. As the ceremony was taking place a figure in a white shimmering gown appeared before 30 witnesses, and touched the young woman on the shoulder before disappearing. The members of the congregation were so much in a state of shock that the vicar called for a special service the following day so that he could offer them some reassurance as to the nature of the apparition.

Although many who claim to have seen the apparition of an angel have stated that the celestial being was no more than a powerful beam of light with no particular form, they had no doubt whatsoever that the phenomenon was an angelic being that had appeared to them in times of sadness. Angels have always been a fact of life, and their appearances do not in any way seem to be dependent on faith or belief in a higher power. By creating an Angels' Book of Promises you will be able to establish a relationship with Angels you can call upon whenever you are in need.

CHAPTER TWO

WHAT IS THE ANGELS'
BOOK OF PROMISES?

The Angels' Book of Promises is quite simply your personal way of keeping a record of things you have asked of the angels as well as the things you are willing to do in return. It is an extremely powerful psychological/spiritual tool that helps with the empowerment of your prayers. It should not be dismissed as 'childish' as its simplicity is what makes it quite special and effective. The Angels' Book of Promises becomes sacred the more it is kept away from other people, and not seen or touched by anyone but you. The book itself becomes the focus of your inner-most desires, dreams, fears as well as your aspirations and endeavours, pretty much in the same way a child keeps a 'secret' diary in which to write his or her personal feelings about their life in general. Once created and empowered, the Angels' Book of Promises becomes an extremely effective method of establishing a relationship with the Kingdom of Angels, so that you can call upon the ones assigned to you when you are in need of help.

CHOOSING YOUR ANGELS' BOOK OF PROMISES BOOK
Once you have decided to create your own Angels' Book of Promises it is important that you take time in choosing the right one for you. It should ideally be a book with a hard cover to ensure it is hardwearing, and must also contain a generous amount of blank pages. Try not to be too hasty in finding the right book, as this will defeat the whole object of the exercise. In fact, in many cases people have said that once they had decided to create their own Angels' Book of Promises the 'perfect' book just seemed to appear from nowhere, perhaps on a shelf in an old

bookshop; or even more bizarrely, given to them by a friend, almost as though the person knew exactly what their gift was going to be used for. You may even decide to use a book you have had for many years; it really doesn't matter where you get your book from as long as you feel it is just right for you. Once you are happy that you have got the empty book you are going to use, set about decorating its cover colourfully so that it really and truly becomes your own. Make the book 'special' in any way you can think of, ensuring that it has your own very private *mark*.

THE LAYING OUT OF YOUR BOOK

It is important not to write in your book right away without preparing it before hand. It needs to be carefully laid out so that you know exactly where and what you are going to write. It is important that the book is divided into sections, and that on one side of the book you write the things you want the angels to do for you, and on the other side what you are willing to do in return. It is as simple as that. You may even decide to create your Angels' Book of Promises in a different way to the one I have explained – it really doesn't matter. The important thing is to personalise your book and make it your own. You may even want to brighten the pages of the book a little by adding a few colourful shapes. You may even design a special symbol, perhaps one that represents you and your relationship with the Angelic Kingdom, and put this on the front of the book, giving it your own personal hallmark. It doesn't matter how crazy the finished book looks as long as it says, 'This is mine!'

CREATING YOUR SACRED SPACE

As with anything of such a sensitive, spiritual nature, the environment in which you work with your Angels' Book of Promises must be pure, clean and fragrant. I am not suggesting that you disinfect everything and fall to your hands and knees and scrub the floor and furniture. On the contrary, a quiet corner of the garden, weather permitting will suffice in which to create your Sacred Space, or simply a quiet room in your home. It is vitally important to the whole empowering process that you are consistent and use the same place each time you enter a request in your Angels' Book Of Promises. In my garden I burn a lantern in front of a large stone Buddha around which I have placed some crystals, primarily to contribute to the whole ambience of my daily meditation ritual. Remember, even if you are not interested in the ritualistic approach to using your Angels' Book of Promises, it is still important to have your own quiet corner of the universe, in fact, your Sacred Space.

Bear in mind, if you do choose a corner of the garden, your use of it may well depend on the weather, and so a covered area would be more suitably practical. I also have a quiet corner in our bedroom, right by the window overlooking the Dee Estuary. The picturesque scene alone helps my mind to be quiet and relaxes me. Because I have always had an affinity with St Teresa, I have a small statue of her on the locker beside my bed where I meditate and pray in front of the window. Even though your use of the Angels' Book of Promises does not necessitate you to be devoutly religious, it is still important to treat the whole process with some respect, pretty much as you would behave walking into a place of worship. The use of incense is ideal for many reasons; apart from allowing a sweet fragrance to permeate your Sacred Space, it also creates the right atmosphere for meditation, as well as keeping flies away from the area. Some incense even produces a hypnotic effect upon the mind, sometimes very helpful where meditation is concerned.

Here are a few suggestions to help you create the correct ambience for your Sacred Space.

- *It is important to keep your Angels' Book of Promises very private. Allowing others to be privy to what you have written in it may dissipate its energy and make its contents less effective.*

- *Write what you are asking for on one page of the book, and what you are willing to do in return on the opposite page. Make certain the writing is in your own very neatest hand, and when writing in the book be very mindful of what you are saying.*

- *Make certain that you are sincere and write from the heart, thus impregnating your words with emotion.*

- *It is important that you do not write without thinking about what you want to say. By choosing your words very carefully are they then released with the force of the emotion with which they were first created, and it is this that perpetuates what you have written. I have said elsewhere that it is important not to write too many requests at once, as this merely causes confusion and defeats the whole object of the exercise.*

- *Before you actually begin using your Angels' Book of Promises as previously explained it is a good idea to sit quietly with it in your hands. Use this quiet time as a means of empowering your book with all the emotional energy you can muster.*

- *Even when you are not calling upon the angels, time permitting, it is important to sit quietly at least twice a day with your book.*

- *Simply hold it gently in your hands, allowing your mind to blend – to merge with it. Feel that you are holding an extremely holy artefact of great significance that nobody else but you have seen.*

- *Spend at least 10 minutes each time just allowing your mind to blend totally with your Angels' Book of Promises.*

- *You should also create a carefully set out space at the back of the book to note unusual things that have happened to you, and which could not really be explained. In this part of the book also make a note of nice people and even animals that have become an integral part of your life. In fact, make a note of everything that you think might be connected in some way to your relationship with Angels. Sometimes it is even a good idea to create a second Angels' Book - perhaps calling this The Angels' Book of Visitors. This can be the book in which to keep a record of everything that has happened to you since you have been using the Angels' Book of Promises.*

- *When you feel ready to place your first entry in the book, this is exactly what you should do.*

THE PROCESS OF PREPARATION

- *Remember, if you choose not to follow the ritualistic approach, you can simply sit quietly whilst writing in your Angels' Book of Promises. Although it must be said, that although still effective, this approach very often takes longer to establish.*

- *If you have chosen a quiet corner of a room in your home, it is a good idea to place a bowl of clear fresh water on a small table in front of you. The water represents purity and clarity of thought, and at the conclusion of your meditation a glass of it should be consumed. Make sure you have an empty glass close at hand.*

- *Place four white or blue lighted candles strategically around the bowl of water. The colour of the candles can either alternate or be all the same. The candles are self-explanatory and represent the spirit and the guiding light of the Divine. For this very reason Angelic beings nearly always relate to a lighted candle.*

- *Burn some pleasant incense, ensuring that you are familiar with the fragrance and know that it is not unpleasant. Incense clears the air and relaxes the mind, a prerequisite for Angelic Rituals.*

- *Place four small pieces of amethyst crystals, one with each candle. Amethyst is often referred to as 'The Spiritual Stone' and will help in the process of purification of the atmosphere in preparation for your prayerful moment. The Amethyst stones do help but are not an essential part of the process.*

You should now be ready to work with your Angels' Book of Promises.

STARTING TO WRITE IN YOUR BOOK

Before writing in your book you must call upon the angels by means of your own special private prayer. This can either be the one I have given below, or one you have created yourself, it really doesn't matter. First of all, take a look at the prayer below and then decide what you want to do.

PRAYER:
O Blessed Messengers of the Divine Light, I call upon you in my time of need, to give me help with my plight and afford me wisdom to succeed in all my endeavours and my dreams; and ask that you will my soul inspire, to raise my heart and mind each passing day, and guide me to all those things to which I aspire. AMEN

The above prayer is a general one asking for help, inspiration and guidance. This prayer should preferably be recited out aloud as opposed to said mentally. The sentiment contained in the words covers virtually everything you need to say. Used regularly over a period of time, it will invoke the appropriate Angelic forces who have either already attached themselves to you, or will be attracted to you because of your particular need or distress. Although prayers may be created for every different need, this is not a necessity. It is true that Angels get to know you by the quality of your thoughts and prayers, but more often than not they will take pains to avoid intruding or presuming that you need their help and will wait until a request is delivered through prayer or entered in your book.

As I have already explained, write your request – whatever you need help with on one side of the book and on the other side write what you are willing to do in return. As I have said, this may sound like a bargaining tool to encourage the Angels to guide you, but it is more to show that you are willing to do something to prove to them that you are not just going to take their help for granted.

When writing in your Angels' Book of Promises you should make it clear what you need. Make certain that you do not ask for several things at the same time, as this adds confusion and may seem as though you are misusing or even abusing their help and taking the whole process light-heartedly. It may take a little time for you to establish a powerful connection with the Kingdom of Angels, but they more than likely know of you already and may be patiently waiting for you to request their help.

Not all Angelic beings have lived in this world of earth, sky and human habitations. Many have never experienced what it is like to live in a physical body and may simply avail themselves to you in the form of an unfolding opportunity, or even a sudden change of circumstance. Occasionally an Angel will come into your life as an ordinary living individual; perhaps someone who will have felt inspired to help you in some way. Do not in any way underestimate the power of the Kingdom of Angels; nothing is beyond their capabilities; nothing whatsoever is beyond their control and reach.

Once you have entered your request and also what you will do in return on the appropriate pages of the book, you must sit quietly with it in your hands for several minutes, allowing what you have written to be processed in your mind. Feel as though the book is almost coming 'alive' with everything you have written in its pages.

You should go through the same process every day if practical, or until such time that you intuitively feel '*rapport*' with the Angelic beings of Light.

Always bear these important points in mind:

- **DO NOT** ask for too many things all at once, as this merely causes some confusion.

- **DO** be clear and concise and try not to make feeble, inane or selfish requests, as these will be looked upon with the contempt they deserve.

- **ALWAYS** be mindful of the Universal Law of Attraction and know that what you send out via your book will come back to you twofold.

When you feel satisfied and are ready to begin the first ritualistic process, close your book and place it as close to the lighted candles as possible, and sit quietly for a few minutes longer. Remember, it is not absolutely essential to practise your first Angel ritual every time you write in your Angels' Book of promises, but a prayer should be an integral part of the process. However, if you feel that the process should always be included in the ritual of writing in the book, and time will permit you to do so, then so much the better. Your Angels' Book of Promises will become more empowered each time you go through this process, and so take care when conducting it.

Cautionary note: Never rush either the process of writing in the book or the ritualistic procedure as this tends to lessen the value of the whole exercise. It is important that your mind is quiet at all times and that you do not feel too tense or stressed.

- *Before bringing the first ritual to a close, spend a few moments breathing rhythmically, ensuring that the inhalations and exhalations are as evenly spaced as possible.*

- *Once you have placed the entries in your book and conducted the appropriate period of sitting quietly, take the book once again in your hands, and then with extended arms hold the book over the flames of the candles, (but not too close) mentally dedicating it to the angels who are watching over you. Allow it to remain in that position for a few moments before returning it to the table.*

- *Finally, carefully extinguish the flames of the candles, pour a short measure of water from the dish into the glass, and then drink it before relaxing.*

You have now made your very first entry in your Angels' Book of Promises, and taken the first steps to establishing your relationship with the Kingdom of Angels.

Although this book offers different rituals and exercises for establishing contact with the Angelic Kingdom, you do not have to use them. Choose the ones that you prefer and which work for you and create your own Angel programme. You may even prefer to modify some of the methods a little to make them work more effectively for you. As long as the programme works for you, do whatever it takes.

As well as being the Key to Self Mastery, meditation is often described as the highest form of prayer, and an extremely effective way of reaching higher states of consciousness, wherein you can access the Celestial Light and the Kingdom of Angels.

CHAPTER THREE

ANGEL MEDITATION

I would not expect for one moment anyone who is sceptical of Angels to even give this book a first never mind a second glance. However, should you be a sceptic and have opened the book at this chapter I would ask you to please read on.

In the 1960s it was quite fashionable to become a devotee of meditation. In fact it was a prerequisite for followers of the 'Flower Power' philosophy, which was *'Peace, Love and Transcendental meditation.'* Fortunately, or unfortunately, whichever way you choose to look at it, I am a refugee of that incredible period, and proud of it! In fact, it was my interest in Yantric Meditation that helped me survive the rigours and traumas of that time and brought me to the point in my life I am at today.

Yantric meditation is the use of geometric shapes or designs. In Buddhism Yantras are referred to as Mandalas – Sacred Patterns or circles that to some externalise *who* and *what* you are. To others they symbolically represent consciousness and are focal points for meditation and contemplation. In fact, a Mandala can take many forms, and may be a simple circle or an intricate geometric pattern on a rug or carpet, or even a complex eastern design created especially with Angel meditation in mind.

Angel meditation is yet another effective way of focusing the attention with the sole purpose of accessing higher states of consciousness. For the purpose of Angel Meditation it is important that you create your own Mandala or Yantra, whatever you choose to call it. Although as I have already said it can be a simple circle design, ideally it should be quite colourful and be comprised of intricate, concentric circles with interwoven patterns. However, in any case you should allow your imagination to play an integral part when creating it.

Once you have decided on your design and have set about creating it, take time in doing so and bear in mind exactly what it is intended for. Make certain that you create it with love and care, and be mindful of the Angelic beings with whom you are endeavouring to connect all through the process. This in itself sends impulses of energy into the universe, an essential part of the whole process.

There are three essential steps to this particular Angel meditation, and each one performs a specific function. You should have already created your sacred space, and used it in the previous ritual. It should already be laid out with the bowl of fresh water, the candles and the amethyst crystal pieces. Of course, you need to decide what course your meditation is to take, and in which order the whole process is to run. I am only giving you an idea how to set about the ritual of Angel meditation, but you may decide on your own ideas. You may even decide not to use a geometric shape in your meditation process. It is entirely up to you whether you integrate the three meditation tools, or use them in separate rituals. Whichever way you decide to do the meditation will be correct for you.

THE THREE STEPS TO ANGEL MEDITATION

- *The first part of the meditation is what I refer to as 'The Initiation' of Your Angels' Book of Promises. Although you have already dedicated your book in the previous exercise, this meditation may well appeal to you more. This is the most important part of the Angel meditation and is the only ritual that MUST be carried out properly. If you have chosen the meditation approach as opposed to the previous exercise, it should be performed in the follow way.*

- *Once you have written in your book what you are asking for and what you are willing to do in return, it should then be dedicated to the Angels in very much the same way as you have done previously.*

- *Dedicate the book by taking it in both hands and then holding it over the bowl of water (not too close to the candles,) and say either mentally or out loud, '***Here is my book which I humbly offer to those who are willing to watch over and take care of me.***' You may feel that you need to change the words to suit you, so do whatever you feel is necessary. When you do this it is vitally important to the whole process that you think about what you are saying and that it is not said mechanically and without thought. Once this has been done, sit quietly for a further five minutes with your book resting gently on your lap, and your eyes closed. During this time endeavour to impregnate the book with your strong desire to contact the Angelic Kingdom, and to establish a relationship with your own personal Guardian Angel.*

- *The second part of the Angels' meditation ritual involves the Mandala. By using the Mandala you are focusing your attention on something you have created specifically with the angels in mind. During Angels' meditation it is important to hold the mind steady and not allow it to wander even for a moment, as this 'interrupts' the connection you are endeavouring to establish with the Angelic Kingdom and defeats the whole object of the exercise. Space permitting, it is a good idea to hang the Mandala on the wall, or perhaps prop it up fairly close to where you are sitting. You need to be able to see it clearly, and whether it is a simple shape or a complicated design if you are going to use the Mandala, it is to be an integral part of the meditation process and should therefore fit in perfectly with everything else. How to use the Mandala will be given later.*

- *The third and final part of the Angels' meditation is a process termed 'Catoptromancy', scrying with a mirror or shiny metal plate. As a child I would use a small mirror placed to my side, and would watch any reflections in it through my peripheral line of vision. As I have already said, you may decide not to use all of the meditation tools at the same time, and may even choose to use the mirror in a separate meditation period. I will explain exactly how to use the Mandala and Angel Mirror in the following chapter.*

You may well be one of those people who find meditation difficult, and may even mistakenly believe that it is only for certain kinds of people and perhaps not necessary to make 'contact' with the Angelic Kingdom. Meditation itself is the highest form of prayer, and is the tool of all great minds. In order to establish contact with those Angelic beings residing in the supersensual side of the universe, it is necessary for the consciousness to be raised, and this can only be achieved through the process of meditation, whichever form that takes. All meditation periods should be preceded and concluded with a period of rhythmic breathing, and should be followed in this way.

First of all, in yoga a pulse beat is referred to as a pulse unit, and as everybody's heartbeat is different, it should be measured in the following way.

- *Ascertain your normal heartbeat by placing your fingers on your pulse, and counting, 1,2,3,4,5,6; 1,2,3,4,5,6 with each corresponding pulse unit.*

- *The units of inhalation and exhalation should always be the same; in this case, six pulse units; whilst the retention and between breaths should always be one half the number of inhalations and exhalations − three pulse units.*

- *Sit in a comfortable position with your eyes closed, ensuring that your chest, neck and head are as nearly in a straight line as possible, with your shoulders thrown slight back.*

- *Once your pulse rhythm has been fully established in your mind, place your hands gently on your lap, palms down, and commence breathing in this way. Inhale very slowly a complete breath, counting six pulse units; hold your breath, counting three; and then exhale slowly (through your nose, but with the lips slightly parted) counting six pulse units; count three pulse units between breaths, and so on.*

- *The majority of people fall into this method of rhythmic breathing quite easily, and even find it very enjoyable. Rhythmic breathing is an essential part of preparing the mind for meditation, and has the effect of slowing everything down, and also helps to decrease the level of thought activity in the brain. Breathing in this way should be maintained for at least ten minutes, but without straining or making it a labour. This method of breathing will also help to calm you down when you are stressed or anxious, and will encourage relaxation in preparation for sleep.*

Angels are immortal spiritual beings and are messengers of God. Although we expect to actually 'see' them, they also have the power to infiltrate our minds and appear to us subjectively during prayer or meditation. They can intervene in our lives at any time they choose, and may lift us from the heaviest burden or traumatic situation at any moment. Angels are highly evolved spiritual beings who choose to guide us through our struggles, sorrows and turbulence. We can quite easily call upon Angels through meditation and magical rituals, but they may also come unbidden into our lives in times of great need. Angels are from a completely different plane of existence, but have the power to infiltrate your life simply by influencing circumstances or causing a chance meeting of a so-called 'Good Samaritan' who has the power to help you.

RECAP OF THE THINGS YOU NEED FOR ANGEL MEDITATION

- *BOWL OF CLEAR WATER; FOUR WHITE OR BLUE CANDLES*

- *A GEOMETRIC DESIGN (MANDALA)*

- *A MIRROR OR SHINY METAL DISC*

- *PLEASANT INCENSE OR FRAGRANT OIL WITH BURNER*

ANGELS' MAGIC RITUAL

To many ordinary thinking people the very mention of 'ritual' where anything of a spiritual nature is concerned, is often off-putting and may suggest anything but a spiritual process. However, where Angel communication is concerned, the ritual employed is of the highest kind, and can only therefore be empowered by the good intentions of the practitioner and whatever feelings he or she carries within their own heart. Ritual is vitally important when endeavouring to make 'contact' with the Angelic Kingdom, and should simply be looked upon as an extension and outward expression of prayer. The other way of looking at this ritual is to see it as a spiritual discipline with the sole object of calling upon angels. The actual ritual is an 'offering' to the Angels and a demonstration of your earnest desire for *them* to come into your life.

Having created your Mandala or geometric shape, you will find that no great effort is required when using this as an integral part of the ritualistic meditation. All that one needs to do is to gaze at its centre and explore every aspect of its intricate (or not) patterns, its lines, curves and overall shape. As the geometric design was created with a specific emotion and desire for Angel communication, the symbol itself should take you on a guided mental journey, and should encourage in you the release of other deeply buried emotions and feelings.

THE GEOMETRIC DESIGN PROCESS (Mandala)

Once you have created and used your meditation ritual several times, you may feel that you need to change things around a little. Should this be the case then just follow your instincts and reorganise the overall layout until you are happy with it. In any case, should you decide to use everything I have explained in the Angel Meditation ritual, the Mandala and the mirror, you should create a space sufficiently comfortable to include everything in the meditation area. The mirror should be free-standing and small enough to be placed on the table to the left of the bowl, and the Mandala should ideally be directly in front of you, but close enough for you to be able to see it clearly.

- *Let us first consider how the Mandala is to be used. Focus your gaze on the centre of the geometric shape, using your peripheral sight to scan the circumference without actually moving your eyes to look at it. You may find this difficult to achieve at first, but practise will bring about positive and amazing results.*

- *At first resist the temptation to blink, or to move your eyes away even for a single moment. When your eyes begin to tear and you can no longer look without clearing them, slowly close your eyes and place the palms of your hands over them, applying slight pressure to your eyeballs.*

- *Within moments the after-image of the Mandala should appear in your mind's eye. Hold it there for as long as you possibly can, and try to determine all you can about the image. It should appear in the opposite complementary colours to what the Mandala actual is. Using the power of your will endeavour to strengthen the image making it more clearly defined. You can do this by breathing in and out a few times, vivifying the image with each inhalation. When it eventually fades and becomes fragmented, open your eyes and return your gaze to the Mandala, and then repeat the exercise again. In fact, repeat this process three or four times, until you have become accustomed to seeing the after-image in your mind's eye.*

- *Once you are familiar with the process of gazing at the geometrically designed Mandala, you should now be ready to attempt using the mirror in the scrying process termed Catoptromancy.*

CATOPTROMANCY AND THE MAGIC MIRROR

Cataptromancy is a form of divination using reflective surfaces, such as a mirror, water or some other suitable surface.

Both the *Magic Mirror* and the *Mandala* may be used individually, by themselves as separate tools for externalising the consciousness. Combined in the ritualistic process of Angel Meditation they form an extremely powerful conduit for Angel energy. Having lit your candles, all natural light should then be eliminated. As long as you don't feel uncomfortable with this, make certain that any light apart from the flickering flames of the candles is subdued.

- *Having familiarised yourself with the whole procedure, situate the mirror on the table or close to it on the left of the bowl, positioned so you can actually see it in your peripheral sight.*

- *Having decided exactly how you are going to conduct the whole ritual, and in which order, simply gaze at the geometric design in front of you, ensuring that the mirror can be seen in the corner of your eye without actually looking at it.*

- *Breathe rhythmically, as before ensuring that the inhalations and exhalations are evenly spaced and that you feel quite comfortable and relaxed.*

- *Gaze at the centre of the Mandala (this time blinking when required,) and whilst staring allow the mirror to be visible in the periphery of your sight.*

- *Occasionally you will find it necessary to focus your attention totally on the Mandala, but always be mindful of the mirror to your side.*

- *Try not to be distracted and to look away to any other part of the room, as this will interfere with the whole scrying procedure, and will defeat the object of the exercise, which is to see and establish contact with Angelic Beings.*

- *Now, you should mentally send out the request for your Guardian Angels to come close. 'Please come close and allow yourself to be seen.' Just a few simple words will suffice, avoiding anxiety or nervousness, as these negative vibrations also interfere greatly with the process.*

- *Be mindful of any unusual anomalies that might appear fleetingly in the mirror, but it is also important to acknowledge whatever you see, either by mentally saying, 'Thank you, I have seen you,' or simply by saying 'Please allow me to feel your presence and benefit from your guidance.'*

- *Regardless of what you see or experience, spend no longer than twenty minutes on the entire ritualistic process, as this will only make you tired and will be unproductive.*

Remember, I am only suggesting ways that you can conduct the meditation ritual, but these can be changed and modified to suit you.

BOWL OF WATER, LIGHTED CANDLES AND AMETHYST STONES

As I have previously said, if you feel uncomfortable with them, there is no need to use the Mandala and the mirror in your Angel Meditation. Although both of these *focusing* tools contribute a great deal of energy to the ritualistic process, the success of the practise is not solely dependent upon their use. The bowl of water and the candles combined are ritualistically complete, and should you prefer they are all you really need when *offering* the Angels' Book of Promises during the sacred process. However, the drinking of some of the water is an essential part of the process, as this symbolically represents the ritual of *'Toasting'* the Angels in the form of a welcome or greeting. All this may sound a little far-fetched and fanciful, but it is a method I have used with some degree of success since I was very young.

As I have previously explained, the Amethyst Pieces are also a matter of choice, although it must be said that these encourage a great deal of energy to be created during the ceremony. I have already explained that Amethyst is referred to as the 'Spiritual Stone', the properties of which are extremely powerful in the manifestation of spiritual forces, and also help to create an immense screen of protection. Although the methods we are exploring in this book are extremely safe and effective, as with all rituals of this nature, occasionally other less spiritually inclined beings are attracted, purely out of curiosity. The candles also represent the spirit and the burning away of negative thoughts, and the water is a symbolic representation of the cleansing of the impure and the washing away of that which is tarnished. The Amethyst pieces polarise the sacred space and encourage a much purer and more spiritualised environment. This does not mean that you will encounter problems if Amethyst pieces are not used in the ritual; on the contrary, you are always the master and in control, and your intentions will always suffice to guide and protect you.

SPIRITUAL YOU AND THE UNIVERSE

We live to all intents and purposes in a multidimensional universe, in which there are worlds within worlds, each rising in a gradually ascending vibratory scale, from those which touch and blend with the highest planes of the physical world, to those which gradually merge with the lowest spheres of the astral world. It is in those lowest spheres that the less spiritually evolved dwell; the vagabonds of the astral world, whose low intelligence and lack of spiritual understanding, prevent them from evolving to the higher more refined planes of consciousness. Although the astral world is not a place, it orbits within and around the physical atom, interpenetrating our world of earthly individuals and physical dwellings. The inhabitants of the lower spheres of the astral world walk through and around us, very often unaware of our presence, just as we are frequently unaware of theirs. Those of us who endeavour to initiate any sort of spiritual metamorphosis within ourselves, unconsciously release a surge of energy that resounds through the universe, its ascending light attracting the attention of all those in the lower spheres. Until you have mastered the technique and feel confident with the process of Angel Meditation, the onus is entirely upon you to take every measure possible to safeguard yourself and to think correct thoughts. Remember, you are only as strong as your lowest thought, regardless of how pure and spiritual your aspirations.

THE AURIC LIGHT

The human organism is an electromagnetic unit of immense power, appropriating, assimilating and releasing energy, and is also contained within its own spectrum of colour and light. As well as being a metaphysical phenomenon, this is also now a scientific fact. The metaphysical spectrum of colour and light emitted from the physical body is referred to as the *Auric Bioluminescence*, the vaporous glow we have come to know simply as 'The Aura.' Bioluminescence is the production and emission of light by a living organism, and is thought to be the result of a chemical reaction during which chemical energy is converted in the cells of the body into light energy. This phenomenon is seen in some aquatic creatures, and in the human organism is an external indication as to the degree of internal balance or imbalance, whichever the case maybe. This subtle 'glow' is also an indication as to the degree of spiritual development attained by the individual, and shines like a beacon to the Kingdom of Angels. The scientists' extensive research into human bioluminescence led them to postulate that there is also a Bio-plasma body interpenetrating the physical body, the emanations of energy from which extend beyond the confines of the visible spectrum. One can assume then that an integral part of man's being manifests in other more refined worlds, at the same time as existing in the so-called visible world. 'What has this got to do with contacting Angels?' I can almost hear you say. In consideration of the nature of invisibility, quite a lot. Angelic beings are able to access and influence the more subtle aspects of our being without actually making physical contact or even showing themselves to us. The aura of each individual is a conduit of spiritual energy and thought, and our intentions are released into the universe like radio or television signals in the atmosphere. I said at the beginning of this book that as a child I used to look upon the universe as a huge cosmic listening device through which the Angels were able to listen to our prayers. And so, the angels would say to us: 'No need for your reports, we know you by the colour of your thoughts.'

As Spiritual beings living in a dense, three dimensional world, we are vulnerable, and that invisible part of our being that extends beyond the confines of the visible spectrum, is constantly being surveyed, watched and scrutinised; not only by angels, but also by those who inhabit the lower spheres of the astral world. Angel Meditation encourages more clarity of thought and trains the mind to be much stronger and more focused in the whole process of establishing contact with the Kingdom of Angels. We are at all times the architects of our own destinies by the way we think; and our thoughts will always attract to us thoughts and *beings* of a similar nature. The more you use Angel Meditation as a means of drawing angels into your life, the purer your thoughts will become. You should eventually see the face of your guardian angel on the shiny surface of your scrying tool, and so keep a record of everything you see and experience.

CHAPTER FOUR

MUSIC, ANGELS
AND THE REALMS OF SLEEP

Researchers looking at the effects of music on the human psyche have concluded that as the human race evolved, music was intricately woven into the lives of virtually every culture around the world. Neuroscientists have stated that music is an integral part of our biological makeup, encoded into our genetic nature as a part of what makes us human. Music is also capable of encouraging memories of our ancestors to surface from our DNA into our consciousness, evoking feelings of 'knowing' and 'seeing' things that we ourselves have never experienced. Studies into the effects of music have in fact shown that it is far more effective than meditation in encouraging both the brain and body to relax. Certain types of soothing music produce theta brainwaves, similar to those in deep relaxation and stage 1 of sleep. In fact, many practitioners of meditation have found certain pieces of music to be more effective in producing states of deep relaxation, particularly during periods of acute stress and anxiety.

Music encourages the release of endorphins in the brain and helps to engage our attention, distracting our thoughts away from worries, stresses and concerns. Music also has an incredible effect upon the supersensual universe, and attracts the interest of Angelic Beings, particularly when we sleep.

Listening to certain types of music whilst thinking of the Kingdom of Angels, just before you retire for the night, allows them to come close. Listening to music at this time encourages the consciousness gently into sleep. It is during the Hypnogogic period - that is when the mind is moving from being awake to actually being asleep - that Angelic beings are able to infiltrate your consciousness. This method of Angel communication is extremely effective and one that appeals to those who do not really have the time to go through the Angel meditation ritual, but do have the time to listen to music before retiring.

- *Spend about forty minutes before retiring relaxing in an armchair listening to some soothing music. The music can be anything from a gentle piece of Baroque, such as Vivaldi or even Purcell, to some so-called 'New Age' meditation music. In fact, anything that encourages the mind and body to relax evokes nostalgic memories to surface in the consciousness.*

- *Whilst listening to the music, write something in your Angels' Book of Promises. You do not have to write something you need help with; it can be a simple request for your Guardian Angels to make their presence felt, either in the form of a lucid dream, or perhaps in an 'Astral-Sleep' experience. The latter is an experience you have when you are asleep that you just know for certain has not been a dream.*

- *Write down your request on one page and on the other what you will do in return to show your appreciation. This can be simply a promise to say a special prayer, or even to light a candle in a show of respect and appreciation.*

- *Allow the music to wash over you, whilst you relax with your book resting gently on your lap. Allow your mind to take you on a nostalgic journey, perhaps back to the happier days of your childhood, slowly following your thoughts forward through the years to the present moment. See how much you have changed, and then express your desire to have the Angels come close to you when you sleep, and even to take you on a spiritual journey of rejuvenation, learning and healing.*

- *Conclude this period with a simple prayer, asking for protection, strength and guidance throughout the night while you sleep, and through each day.*

- *If you prefer you can use the following example.*

ANGELS' PRAYER FOR SLEEP

Blessed Ones who dwell in the Higher Realms of Light, be vigilant as you watch over me all through the night; I pray that I might experience your touch whilst I sleep, and feel secure that you will my soul in safety keep, away from harm and a restless, fearful night, and ask that you always watch me from the Higher Realms of Light. Amen.

Although a connection can be established quite spontaneously with Angelic Beings, and occasionally without any great effort, it usually takes time and a great deal of patience before positive results can be achieved. As I have stated in an earlier chapter, Angels very often influence the circumstances of your life, as opposed to appearing to us or making their presence felt. Establishing a relationship with the Angelic Kingdom should not be done purely out of curiosity, or to simply see if you can do it. There should always be a valid reason, and an incorrect motive sends the wrong single through the supersensual universe to the Angels' Realms of Light.

- *Before snuggling down beneath the warm covers to go to sleep, lie for a few moments, on your back, staring at a selected point on the ceiling.*

- *Focus your attention on that point for five minutes, and commence breathing rhythmically, as before ensuring that the inhalations and exhalations are evenly spaced.*

- *Conclude the rhythmic breathing by mentally saying, 'O Blessed beings of Divine Light, watch over me and keep me safe through the night.' Then allow sleep to naturally wash over you.*

I have explained in an early chapter that man is an extremely complex being. He has seven bodies, each one rising in a gradually ascending vibratory scale, and each comprised of a much finer material than the one below it, and so on. When we sleep the consciousness is slowly passed from the physical body into the next vehicle of astral matter, where it experiences awareness at that particular level. It is there that we usually encounter the spirits of our 'dead' relatives and friends, and although we rarely have any memory of this upon awakening, the experience is firmly established in the subliminal areas of our consciousness. During sleep, whilst the consciousness is slowly ascending, we are watched over by other spiritual beings that have become known by the very fashionable term of 'Spirit Guides' or helpers. These discarnate beings are supervised by the more highly evolved Angels of Light, a Supreme Hierarchy with the responsible relentless task of watching over humanity. Sceptics always ridicule the fact that Spirit Guides are nearly always depicted as Native Americans, monks or nuns, and never simple workmen. The answer to this always seems to be that these discarnate individuals were either closer to the earth or just simply far more spiritually evolved. The truth is the way in which so-called Spirit Guides present themselves to mediums and other psychically inclined individuals is quite misleading and a lot more complex than the majority realise. Some schools of thought believe that so-called Spirit Guides are merely facets of a medium's spiritual personality and as he or she evolves, so another facet manifests in his or her consciousness. We humans always need form and image to relate to. We seem to have some difficulty accepting the fact that our Spirit Helpers may well just be pure energy, and really only manifest as Native Americans etc because that's what we humans expect. We know full well that our egos would not allow us to accept the assistance of a Spirit Guide who had once been a manual labourer, or even a milkman whilst living in the physical world. We look for and expect more exciting and romantic Spiritual individuals to watch over and guide us. This somehow makes us feel more protected and much more important. In fact, little do you realise that more often than not, your Spirit Guide, *Running River*, or whatever you have chosen to call him, may really have been an ordinary workman or woman who has chosen to humour you by taking on the guise of a Native American. I am not suggesting for one moment that no so-called 'Spirit Guides' are Native Americans; on the contrary, many of these highly evolved individuals were closer to the earth and the sun and do come with your best interests at heart. However, what I am saying is that we should accept their help whoever they are and whatever they were when they once lived on this earth. Creation does not in any way stop at man. We are in fact surrounded by invisible beings far superior than us. And it would seem that only in times of great sorrow and need do we acknowledge their presence. We only ever seem to fall to our knees and pray either when someone tells us that a Supernatural Being is close by, or when we are in need of help and guidance. We should always live our lives and behave as though we are in the presence of one who is Holy and Divine, and not wait until it is far too late to prove just how loyal and sincere we really are. A mystic once said:

'Are the Divine recollections that slumber in your soul only to be awakened by the lance thrusts of grief? The wise man and the sage need no such violent arousing. They see a tear, a kindly gesture, a drop of water that falls; they listen to a passing thought, press a brother's hand and approach an infant's smile with open eyes and open soul. They never cease to behold that of which you have caught

but a passing glimpse; and a smile will tell the wise man and the sage all that it took misfortune or the hand of death to reveal to you.

'It behoves you to be keenly vigilant, and better had you watch in the market place than slumber in the temple; for beauty and grandeur are everywhere, and it takes but an unexpected incident to reveal them to you. But it is only when misfortune or death lash at your heart that you grope around the wall of life in search of the crevices through which you might perceive your God! You know full well that there are such eternal crevices even in the walls of a humble hovel; and the smallest window cannot take away a line or a star from the immensity of heavenly space. It is not enough that you possess truth; it is essential that the truth should always possess you. Be quite certain that the day you linger to follow a ray of light through a crevice in the wall of life that you have already done something as great as though you had tended the wounds of your enemies; for from that day on no longer shall you have enemies.'

To acknowledge and not to deny the very existence of Angelic Beings, perpetuates their love and draws them closer to us.

Music is a great healing balm, and a sequence of vibrations essential to the manifestation of Angels in our lives.

It is little known but there are angels of music whose job it is to inspire musicians to compose beautiful masterpieces. Many composers were known to have believed that they were in fact inspired by angels. George Frederick Handel 1685 - 1759, believed that he was inspired by Angelic powers during the composing of the oratorio The Messiah in 1742. Peter Llich Tchaikovsky, 1840-1893, composer of the Romantic era, also claimed to be inspired by Divine Angelic Forces. Joannes Brahms, 1833-1897, composer of four symphonies and a German Requiem in 1868 was a believer that Angels were an integral part of his inspiration. Ludwig Van Beethoven, 1770-1827, composer of Symphonies and Chamber pieces confided in friends that he felt he had guardian angels who were responsible for his inspirations.

CHAPTER FIVE

ANGELS' GESTURES
AND THE MAGIC MIRROR

The incredible interest today in Angels is a clear indication that the planet as a whole is currently passing through a very important Spiritual Epoch, and an age in which the entire human race is struggling towards the *light*, rather like an immense white swan whose wings are flapping noiselessly across the surface of a great ocean. There are times in all our lives when we just cannot ignore the fact that it is not mere chance but something far greater that has pulled us more than once from the painful and miserable circumstances with which we have been faced. I have long since reached this conclusion after being rescued on many, many occasions from dire circumstances and near death situations. I have never been one for mentally harbouring fanciful notions of Angelic Beings taking my hand and leading me to safety through the darkness of a rocky terrain. Even though I risk being mocked, the truth is that's exactly how it has been for me, and I am not in the least bit embarrassed for saying so. Even as a child I suppose I was looked upon by many people as being quite unusual and even 'odd'. 'No change there then!' I can almost hear my mother say, shaking her head in exasperation, and my father adding, 'I told you so, didn't I? What is going to become of him?' Although seeing so-called 'dead' people has always been commonplace to me, my mediumistic skills still had to be cultivated and refined. I have always been regarded as quite radical in my approach to esoteric and metaphysical subjects, and so it was no surprise to those who knew me well that I had no desire to follow the conventional path of development and training. Although I sat in a so-called 'development circle' under the supervision of an elderly medium by the name of Sylvia Alexio, against this wise old lady's wishes I also sat alone for at least one hour every night. My methods were a little unusual to say the least. I employed various scrying techniques and would sit sometimes for hours enthralled by the things I could see. After opening my scrying session with a prayer, I then used an 'Angels' Gesture' (Mudra) I had been shown as a young boy. It was explained to me that this particular hand position would always be recognised by the angels watching over me. I had been using these methods for about six months with some startling results. Suddenly though, for some reason I could not fathom, the things I was 'seeing' in the crystal ball changed dramatically from picturesque and surreal landscapes and anonymous faces, to Angelic Beings of Light. As well as seeing these across the reflective surface of the crystal ball, they also began to manifest in the periphery of my sight, away from the crystal ball. However, when I swung my head round to look directly at them they just disappeared. As I was totally unprepared for these sorts of phenomena, at first it made me quite nervous forcing me to abandon the practise for a few days. Unable to ignore my curiosity for any longer than a couple of days, I began scrying again. This time, though, I decided to use a mirror as my scrying tool, propped up in front of me with a lighted candle either side. I was curious to know who these beings of light actually were, and wanted to know if they were going to help me with my work. Although I was still somewhat apprehensive, I locked the door to ensure I was not disturbed, turned off the lights and lit the two candles. Things became apparent within a very short time, and not only was I now able to see these Beings of Light very clearly in the mirror, but I could now also see them standing behind me in the flickering light of the candle. Although I felt quite nervous I resisted the overwhelming temptation to abandon the practise for a second time. I was overwhelmed by curiosity to continue and was very soon fascinated by the kaleidoscope of colour that seemed to issue from the mirror, filling the candlelit room with a display of all different kinds of gyrating coloured light anomalies. Although I had not been burning any incense I was overwhelmed by a sweet fragrance that permeated the whole room. I decided then to suspend the scrying period and turn on the lights. To my amazement there was a film of iridescent pink powder across the surface of the small table and all round the mirror. There were also traces of it on the face of the mirror itself. Upon closer examination I was able to ascertain that it was the powder that had provided the sweet fragrance. I then realised that the eerie phenomena were most definitely Angelic Beings of Light, and that I had somehow stumbled on an even easier way of attracting them into my life.

Although as a child I frequently amused myself by gazing into a mirror (against my mother's wishes) intrigued by the unusual things I could see, I really only began using a crystal ball as a scrying tool in the mid 1970s, when I was given my grandmother's very old crystal ball and stand. Although I have explored the phenomenon of the Magic Mirror (as I call it) in an earlier chapter, combining its use with the Angels' Finger Gesture (mudra) and candles is far more practical than using a crystal ball as a scrying tool, and can be carried out in the following way.

First of all let me explain about the *Angels' Finger Gesture* and why they are used and also how they are to be properly applied. Mudras, as they are known in eastern yogic traditions, are hand and finger gestures that symbolically channel energy flow through body. To an observer they represent different spiritual attitudes and states of feeling; to the practitioner they are an expression of these attitudes and feeling states.

Although there are only two finger gestures that are to be considered primarily for the purpose of contacting Angelic

Beings of Light, a further two more traditional ones may be used once a firm relationship with the Angelic Kingdom as been established. The latter two finger gestures (or Mudras) have been used for thousands of years by yogic and Buddhist masters primarily as disciplines during the practise of meditation, and signify 'Giving' and 'Fear not', both of which may be used to give specific indications to the angels when they are close. But first let us take a look at the finger gestures with which to precede and conclude the scrying exercise. These are extremely easy to replicate and are ones I have always used as symbols of warmth, love and gratitude.

ANGELS' FINGER GESTURE I

- *Not long after the crucifixion of Jesus the disciples went into hiding for fear of being caught. Before the cross became a recognised Christian symbol the followers of Jesus identified each other by scraping the shape of a fish on the wall. This was also replicated by crossed fingers, the middle finger over the index finger. This in fact is where crossing fingers for good luck originated. The first Angels' Gesture or finger position is based on that symbolic gesture.*

- *Cross the middle finger of both hands over the index fingers.*

- *Now gently place the ring finger of both hands more or less parallel with the middle finger ensuring that the tip of this finger lightly touches the nail of your index finger.*

- *Finally, allow your thumb to lightly touch the tip of you index finger.*

- *Make sure that the completed finger configuration is not uncomfortable, and that you can sit with your fingers in that position for a few moments with both hands placed gently on your lap. This Angel Finger Gesture represents 'Love', 'Friendship' and 'Honour'.*

- *I'm not suggesting that you maintain the Angels' Gesture until the conclusion of the scrying period. Both hands should only be held in this position for the duration of the opening prayer (as given in an earlier chapter,) and then you should simply sit with your open palms down on your lap.*

ANGELS' FINGER GESTURE 2

- *This particular finger position should be used at the conclusion of the scrying period, and should only be maintained for no longer than a minute.*

- *Using both hands simply extend both your middle and index fingers parallel to each other, whilst securing the other two fingers down with your thumb.*

- *Next, place the extended fingers of the right hand across the fingers of your left hand to form an X. It is as simple as that. This represents peace and tranquillity.*

- *At the conclusion of the scrying period simply sit quietly for a minute with the finger configuration resting gently on your lap.*

That is all there is to it! The Angels' Finger Gestures may also be used by themselves; one to precede your meditation period, and the other to conclude it. Using them frequently will empower them so that they can be used as symbols of discipline to relax your mind. Any time you feel tense, anxious or worried about something, simply create the Angels' Finger Gesture of your choice and close your eyes. Once they have been empowered through frequent use, you may find that you can call upon their power at any time you are in need of it. I have also found that they are effective when seeking help from those who are watching over and protecting me.

The two more traditional Finger Gestures I mentioned earlier, that represent 'Giving' and 'Fear not' are frequently seen in medieval paintings of saints or Buddha and may be used at any time during Angel meditation. Once you feel quite confident and are in no doubt that you have established an efficient way of working with the angels, either or even both of these Mudras may be used as a means of expressing your desires to Angelic Beings of Light as they draw close. Remember, if you are anxious or for any reason feeling angry with something in your life, these negative impulses prevent any Angels from coming close. These Mudras may be used to reassure *them* of your intentions, and allows them to breakdown the vibrations of your negative emotions. Let us first of all take a look at 'Giving'. This may be used to allow the Angels looking after you to know that you are giving them your love and your total trust.

THE GIVING MUDRA

The left hand should be resting in the centre of the body, with the palm up, while the right hand should be resting over the right knee but with the palm turned out, thumb and forefinger touching. Pure positive feeling radiates from the open right hand and will encourage the restoration of peace and harmony.

This mudra radiates extremely powerful energies that approaching angelic forces will identify as a clear sign of peace.

THE MUDRA OF FEAR NOT

This mudra sends out positive vibrations also, and will reassure both you and the angels working with you that all is well. Both mudras also serve as disciplines for the purpose of meditation and encourage the creation of positive energies.

The left hand should be resting receptively on your lap, palm facing upward, and the right hand should be raised up to the level of the heart, palm facing out, offering the gesture 'Fear Not!' It is believed that this mudra is an ideal method of non-verbal communication in states where words are inadequate. This mudra also promotes peace and reassurance to all angel visitors.

THE MAGIC MIRROR

Although we have briefly covered the Magic Mirror in a previous chapter, I need now to explore its use in a different way. Those of you who are students of esoteric matters will most probably be familiar with scrying as a means of focusing the mind. In fact, it is an ideal tool for cultivating the faculties and activating the image-making faculty of the brain, a prerequisite for anyone seeking to develop psychic abilities. However, although this book is not about such development, the same tools are used to cultivate awareness of Angelic Beings of Light and also to create a portal, so to speak, through which they can travel into this world. Although strictly speaking Angelic Beings do not require such a portal to enter our physical environment, the process of scrying can attract them very quickly into your life.

Although strictly speaking any mirror will do for the Angel Scrying process, ideally it should measure about 12inches by 10 inches with its own stand to ensure its security. Once used for the purpose of scrying, the mirror should be kept away from natural sunlight and other bright artificial lighting. You should never allow anyone else to see or handle it, and when it is not in use it should be wrapped in a black cloth. This may sound a little mysterious or even strange to you, but it ensures that it is free from the personal vibrations of other people and that it really belongs to you. In this way do you empower the mirror making it your own personal scrying tool.

Before using the mirror you should first make sure it is clean, ensuring that it does not possess any negative vibrations. Once this has been achieved you should sit quietly holding it in both hands, impregnating it with your own personal energies, intentions and desires. This part of the procedure is extremely important to ensure that it is pure and that it will work efficiently. Above all, the mirror must be treated with respect and with some degree of reverence.

MAGIC MIRROR SCRYING

- *Place the mirror in a secure position on the table in your Sacred Space and then place a candle either side of it.*

- *It is important that you allow the same piece of music to play each time you practise the process of Angel Scrying, as this will eventually become a sort of signal of recognition to those whom you are calling. Make certain however that the music is not too loud and is an emotionally stirring piece.*

- *Unlike the previous method where you only saw the mirror in your periphery line of vision, this time you should look directly into it.*

- *Before lighting the candles it is a good idea to say a short prayer for guidance and protection.*

- *Light the candles and then sit comfortably in your chair, ensuring that the mirror is perfectly in line with your eyes.*

- *Gaze at your reflection in the mirror, ideally at the spot between your brows.*

- *Make sure that you are nice and relaxed, and that your breathing is slow and rhythmical.*

- *For the first five minutes resist the temptation to blink or to move your gaze away from the mirror even for a moment.*

- *When your eyes begin to tear and you can gaze no longer, close them and place the palms of your hands over your eyes, applying slight pressure to the eyeballs.*

- *Allow the after-image to appear in your mind, and using the power of your will, maintain it for as long as you possibly can. When it begins to fade, open your eyes and return you gaze to the mirror and repeat the exercise. This time though blink when necessary, but do not move your gaze from the mirror.*

- *The reason you had to close your eyes for the first part of the exercise is primarily to activate the image-making faculty of the brain. In fact, every time you practise scrying you should always initially resist the temptation to blink for as long as you can, and then close your eyes for as long as the after-image remains on the screen of your mind. The benefits of this are immense and contribute an awful lot to the process of scrying.*

- *There is always the tendency at this point for the practitioner to lose heart and abandon the practise. Persistence and patience are the key words where scrying is concerned, and you must also be observant and make a mental note of any 'unusual' anomalies.*

- *All through the practise it is important to be mindful of the exercise, and to constantly remind yourself of what it is you are endeavouring to achieve. You may in fact experience other phenomena completely unrelated to Angels, and although these may be of interest to you they should be quickly dismissed, and blinking your eyes several times should clear the surface of the mirror.*

- *Angelic Beings of Light very often first begin to manifest as pinpoints of light that gradually metamorphose into long shafts of light. Although you may not actually see any features, you should be able to see clearly defined forms of light.*

- *It may well be that all that you will ever see in the mirror is your own face transfiguring into different forms; should this be the case then you can accept that as an indication that you should abandon the exercise until next time.*

Of course, this method of scrying with the sole intention of attracting Angelic Beings does not suit everybody. I would suggest that you try it at least once if only for the experience. You may well be one of those people who achieve successful results immediately.

Cautionary note: Always remove contact lenses before any scrying exercise as problems can occur with tearing.

All through my life I have wanted to know why some people have transcendental experiences, and why others dismiss such things as ridiculous and absurd. In fact, once I had fully recovered from my dark period of drug addiction, I desperately needed to know what as a child had made my brain different to so many other children my age, and what mechanism in my brain made it possible for me to actually see images of the so-called 'dead', have conversations with them and also be visited by angels. I questioned psychologists, psychiatrists, doctors and even priests, but nobody could come up with an answer that made any sense to me. I really did feel extremely different and even wondered if I had sustained some neurological damage with my years of drug abuse that somehow caused these transcendental experiences to be heightened. It got so bad that I began to doubt my own sanity and did not know where to turn for the answers to the thousands of questions that had been buried so deeply within my brain since I was a child. All I knew was that all the things I had always experienced were very real to me, but at that point in my life I had never met anyone else who had experienced the same phenomena. Wanting to know more, my investigations led me to discover some very significant neurological facts, which then helped me to fully understand the working of the human brain and exactly why psychically inclined individuals experience the phenomena they do.

CHAPTER SIX

TRANSCENDENTAL EXPERIENCE AND THE BRAIN

In 1903, neuroscientist professor Ivan Tutinsky from Moscow University became so fascinated with how the human brain functions during transcendental experience, that he went to stay in a Tibetan Monastery to study the monastic approach to meditation and other transcendental phenomena. Tutinsky wanted desperately to find out exactly why some people had transcendental experiences – one of which being encounters with angels – and others did not. Tutinsky was particularly interested in why some children had encounters with angels and other disembodied experiences. Although the notable professor took pains to avoid the word 'psychic' he was convinced that some sort of malfunction occurred in the brains of those who had such transcendental experiences, and also suggested that such people may even include sufferers of temporal-lobe epilepsy. On his return from Tibet professor Tutinsky devoted seven years of his life writing about his findings. He was willing to compromise his professional integrity and as a result was ridiculed by his peers for his interest in a subject that at the time was viewed with some disdain and cynicism. Nonetheless, professor Tutinsky stood by his neurological studies which he published in a paper for his fellow scientists.

THE PINEAL GLAND

Tutinsky concluded that the pineal gland - a pine-shaped organ deep within the brain, and one of the endocrine glands that secretes melatonin, was in actual fact much larger in a child than in an adult, and more developed in a female than in a male. This he concluded was the very reason why children have far more transcendental experiences than adults and why women have a greater propensity to such experiences than men. Tutinsky went on to say that in his opinion the crystalline deposits around the pineal gland radiated electromagnetic waves, thus causing a disturbance in the multisensory processing network of the brain. He further affirmed that in some cases of temporal lobe epilepsy transcendental visions were experienced during a seizure, and many sufferers claimed to have seen *Angels* and other disembodied apparitions. Today scientists believe that they have discovered the module in the brain responsible for 'God-Consciousness', and they have now also concluded that St Paul's experience of the so-called 'Blinding Light' on the road to Damascus was caused by an epileptic seizure. Whatever was the cause of St Paul's experience there is very little doubt that it caused him to undergo an incredible spiritual transformation.

EXTRAORDINARY POWERS AND EASTERN TRADITIONS

From time immemorial the belief that attaining higher states of consciousness would encourage the cultivation of extraordinary powers has been embraced by many cultures. Some Eastern traditions have always advocated the disciplines of yoga as an effective way of developing psychic powers, or '*Siddhis*' as they known in Eastern philosophy, and others have recommended various forms of meditation to reach *Samadhi*, a state of consciousness that lies beyond waking, dreaming and deep sleep. Whilst in that transcendental state all mental activity ceases and union with God is established. This encourages a pure connection with the Kingdom of Angels and produces a transcendental experience that cannot in anyway be described with words. More often than not, an encounter with Angelic Beings of Light manifests as an experience that transcends the bounds of sensory experience, and although no visible contact takes place, the individual is left in no doubt that an Angel has touched his or her life.

HALLUCINOGENS, TRANSCENDENTAL EXPERIENCE AND ANGELS

Although the disciplines of yoga and meditation have been used successfully for thousands of years, a small minority chose a much quicker route to the *Kingdom of Angels*. This involved the practice of imbibing hallucinogenic substances to produce transcendental states. Although the use of such mind-expanding substances was in the majority of cases, integrated into the culture's religious rituals, such practises were in fact extremely dangerous. The hallucinogens were derived from a variety of naturally occurring plants, from Amanita Muscaria, the so-called Magic Mushroom used in Shamanic rituals, to Mescaline, extracted from the button-shaped nodules of the Mexican Peyote spineless cactus, frequently used by Aztec priests. Another was Psilocybin, a crystalline hallucinogen, also obtained from the so-called *Sacred Mushroom,* used by an ancient mystical sect known as *'The Mushroom People'*, whose whole spiritual philosophy was based on the hallucinogenic properties of the mushroom. In fact, hallucinogens have been an integral part of many spiritual cultures, and some even referred to the hallucinogenic substances they used as the *'Nectar of the Gods'*, as the substance they imbibed allowed them to experience prophetic visions and also have brief encounters with Angelic Beings of Light. Whilst there can be no doubt that the hallucino-genic substances did produce the altered states of consciousness required to make contact with Angelic Beings of Light, those who regularly imbibed the mind-expanding substances frequently sustained permanent brain damage consistent with such use. Even today some religious cultures still depend on hallucinogens to produce euphoric or transcendental states, although now these are mostly in a minority and in the less developed primitive cultures of the world. Nonetheless, the use of hallucinogenic substances does have a powerful effect up on the less active areas of the brain, producing altered states of consciousness and extended awareness on all levels of sensory experience.

NOSTRADAMUS AND ANGELS

The famous French *Seer* and clairvoyant, Nostradamus, (1503-1566) whose prophecies caused controversy for hundreds of years, also imbibed a herbal narcotic to induce a trance-like state. Whilst in this altered state of consciousness Nostradamus had glimpses of future events which he claimed were given to him by Beings of light. Nostradamus was born Michael de Notredame on the 14th December 1503 in St Remy, France to Jewish parents who had in fact converted to Catholicism. He studied the mysteries of the Kabbalah and the prophecies of the Old Testament and claimed to have visions of Angels from a very early age.

OTHER FAMOUS PEOPLE AND ANGELS

It would seem that the belief in angels is not dependent upon religious persuasion. On the contrary, after the death of his son, Raymond, English physicist Oliver Lodge devoted part of his work to scientifically proving the existence of a Spirit World, and also stood by his convictions when he openly admitted that he believed in angels and an after-life. In fact, Oliver Lodge was not afraid to publically declare that he had encountered angels and also met his 'dead' son in a very lucid dream. Although his views were looked upon by his peers with some scepticism, Oliver Lodge's beliefs persisted until the day he died.

Arthur Conan Doyle, the creator of Sherlock Holmes, also believed in angels and an after-life. Doyle in fact went to great lengths to promote his beliefs, and although he was greatly disappointed in the so-called Cottingley fairy photographs, his interest in such matters persisted all through his life.

Alexandra Dumas, author of many books, also allegedly had a belief in angels and attributed his success to a force not of this world.

Maurice Maeterlinck, nineteenth century dramatist and mystic, had a great belief in angelic forces and wrote many essays on mysticism and other related subjects, which he attributed to Angelic inspiration.

Robert Louis Stevenson (1850-1894), author of Treasure Island and many other bestselling books, was an avid believer in Angelic Forces and claimed to have had many encounters with Angelic Beings of Light.

Lewis Carrol (1832-1898) real name Charles Lutwidge Dodgson, the creator of Alice in Wonderland, also believed in Angels and said that he was inspired by some spiritual force and had always felt that he was guided spiritually where his writing was concerned.

Charles Dickens (1812-1870) believed in Angels and their intervention in times of great need.

Mark Twain (1835-1910) real name Samuel Langhome Clemens, creator of Huckleberry Finn and Tom Sawyer, once said that he felt Angelic Beings of some sort were always there in his life.

Herbert G Wells (1866-1946) the creator of the Time Machine and many other bestselling books, also attributed his inspired works to some divine force, and believed that he did have a guardian angel.

Today there seems to be an incredible interest in Angels and Angel communication. In fact, although the concept of angels is extremely fashionable, by their very nature there can be no 'experts' on the subject, even though many claim to be just that. All I am doing is relating my own experiences to you and helping you to explore the methods and techniques that have always worked for me. The Angels' Book of Promises has always been very personal to me, and it is only because of the great interest today in angels that I have decided to share my thoughts with you.

Throughout antiquity all those who have claimed to work with angels have used their own methods to make contact with them. The Angels' Book of promises has always been my own unique way of establishing and maintaining a relationship with Angelic Beings, and although it is open to interpretation, I do know that it will always work as effectively for you as it always has for me.

One piece of advice that was given to me many years ago is, if it is worth having it is worth working for. Results from the Angels' Book of Promises are achieved quicker with some people than others. Why that is I have never known. All that I can say is it is of paramount importance that you explore all the different methods in this book in order to discover the one that works best for you.

The Angels' Book of Promises is much more than an effective psychological tool for establishing a relationship with angels; it is a book with a powerful philosophical content that will in time enhance and change your life in many different ways. I base this purely on my own experience and also know that it has transformed the lives of many people who have learnt how to use the Angels' Book of Promises in my workshops worldwide.

CHAPTER SEVEN

ANGELS IN THE LIVES OF PEOPLE

The majority of incredibly successful people nearly always attribute their success to the help and guidance of either some Divine Power or even Angels. John Lennon once said that when he was writing his songs it sometimes felt as though some disembodied force was involved in the 'inspirational' process. Although John was not particularly religious in a conventional sense, he most certainly acknowledged the fact that he was somehow guided by a power that was not of this world.

Cary Grant once said that he owed his success to the guidance of Angels, and even on-screen gangster, James Cagney once said that he had no doubt that he had a Guardian Angel who was always there when needed.

One of the last men to escape unhurt from the 9/11 World Trade Centre, Twin Towers disaster claimed that he was encouraged by an Angel to push his way down the stairs and through the flames. Each time he faltered he said that the Angel urged him to carry on through the flames and smoked filled building to safety. And Charles Lindbergh, the first man to fly solo non-stop across the Atlantic in 1927 was reputed to have said that he was accompanied on the flight by ghostly apparitions who kept him awake when he struggled with tiredness.

Elvis Presley once said that he believed he was guided by angels and that he owed his success chiefly to some Divine intervention. Antarctic explorer Sir Edward Shackleton said that an unseen presence accompanied him and his three exhausted companions on their return to civilization. Many of those who have successfully climbed Mount Everest claimed that there was a presence with them all the time and that this presence stood close by instructing them exactly what to do.

My own Aunty Louise an ambulance driver with the police through the Second World War was guided through the war torn streets of London by a Being of Light who walked ahead of the ambulance during the blackout. Although my Aunty Louise was also a medium, the Being of Light was also seen by her companion, Sergeant Wells.

In 1995 over 300 people were killed when a department store collapsed in Seoul, Korea. A 19 year old clerk miraculously survived for sixteen days in an air pocket, and when she was rescued she claimed that a ghostly monk had visited her several times, giving her an apple and encouraging words on each occasion.

During the latter part of the Second World War, a Wellington Bomber had sustained extensive damage during an air raid over France; with all the electrics down the crew were unable to navigate the plane through the darkness. With all hope of landing the huge craft safely gone, the crew prepared themselves for the worst. As the plane began to lose altitude the pilot noticed an intense white light shining brightly ahead through the darkness. The unusual light anomaly seemed to suddenly exert an immense power over the plane's failing engines and somehow helped the craft to right itself, with a sudden surge of power. The crew were amazed when the plane's altitude increased. The light persisted through the darkness, holding the damaged plane on a steady course all the way home to England where it was able to land safely. The pilot and crew swore that the plane was miraculously pulled through the air and lowered safely to the ground by some powerful force – a force, they all said, 'was not of this world.'

A young Liverpool mother was terrified when she looked through the kitchen serving hatch to see a ball of fire. Thinking a fire had broken out in the kitchen she dashed from the room to investigate, only to witness an incredible sight. She stood watching, enthralled as the ball of fire gradually metamorphosed into an Angelic Being of Light before finally disappearing before her eyes. The incredible phenomenon transformed the young woman's life and made her more aware of Angels and all things spiritual.

Lost in the depths of despair after her boyfriend had died suddenly of a heart attack, twenty year old Barbara Sands was sitting at the table in her living room crying when she noticed a strange reflection in the mirror. Her heart missed several beats when she saw a beautiful angelic being bathed in a golden light standing behind her. However, when she swung her head round quickly to confront whoever it was, there was absolutely nobody there. A sweet fragrance permeated the room, and then she noticed a film of iridescent pink powder across the surface of the table she was sitting at. She suddenly felt overwhelmed with a sense of peace, and at that moment she knew that her Guardian Angel had come to reassure her that her beloved Michael was all right. The pink iridescent powder seems to be a common phenomenon when angelic apparitions occur.

Ted McCoy had spent his whole life in and out of prison, and now at the age of 61 his future looked bleak. He had been given an 18 month prison sentence for theft, and although he wanted so much to make a break from his old habits, circumstances prevented him from doing so. It was six weeks before Christmas and Ted sat alone in his cell silently contemplating his future alone. His wife had divorced him four years ago, and his two daughters had disowned him completely. As far as Ted was concerned he now had nothing whatsoever to live for. He had no sooner taken the decision to end it all when an extremely bright light filled his cell. The light was so bright he could scarcely see anything. Within moments his eyes became accustomed to the glare and he could distinguish the form of an Angelic presence. The figure remained in his cell for what seemed like an eternity, and the next thing he knew it was morning. Whatever it was that appeared to Ted McCoy it changed his life completely. Today he lives with his second wife, Mary, and has happily settled down to a life free of crime.

Staunch Catholic, Jenny Mower was absolutely devastated when her best friend, Sandra, died suddenly of a brain haemorrhage. They had known each other since they were children, and Sandra's tragic death now made jenny question her faith and belief in God. It was two weeks after the funeral and Jenny had spent a quiet hour in her church prayerfully seeking the answer as to why her friend had died at the age of thirty seven. Although she left the church feeling somewhat despondent, that night exhausted she fell into a deep sleep. She dreamt that she was in a beautiful garden where she was visited by her friend and an Angel attired in a white shimmering gown. In the dream Sandra embraced Jenny and told her not to worry that she was happy. As Sandra said her tearful goodbyes, the Angel sprinkled a handful of glitter over the two friends, and almost at that moment Jenny's husband woke her with a cup of tea and some toast. As she went to tell him about the beautiful dream he interrupted her. 'What's this?' He leaned across and brushed silver glitter from her hair. 'Glitter! Where did that come from?'

A tear rolled down Jenny's cheek, and she muttered almost soundlessly. 'Angel's glitter from heaven.'

These are just a small portion of the many true stories about Angels and the way they have affected people's lives.

CHAPTER EIGHT

THE PSYCHOLOGY OF ANGELS
AND NATURE SPIRITS

A belief in Angels is really down to the individual and is personal and something that is rarely spoken of for fear of ridicule. As I explained at the beginning of this book, although I have had contact with Angels in one form or another since I was a child, I have always been reluctant to speak about my experiences, let alone write about them. I finally decided to voice my opinions when I realised that there was a great interest in Angels and it had in fact become quite fashionable to talk about them. I suppose one could say that I am jumping on the proverbial bandwagon and that I am exploiting the subject in some way. However, I do not profess to be an expert in Angel psychology and I really cannot understand how some writers on the subject claim to be so. How can anyone be an expert on the subject of Angels, when to most they are creatures of conjecture, mythology and religious belief? Everything that I am writing about in this book is based totally on my own experiences and techniques that have worked for me since I was a young boy.

Whether or not Angels come within the parameters of what is termed 'Paranormal' is really a matter of opinion. Nonetheless, parapsychologists are more interested in why some people believe in Angels rather than what Angels actually are and if they really do exist.

Like most children I used to see faces and other unusual shapes in the patterns on curtains and carpets, and was forever being chastised by my mother for spending more time than was good for me making my eyes go out of focus so I could see the images more clearly. This phenomenon is perhaps more common than you might realise, but when I saw them as a child they were quite animated and would respond to me. It is the general consensus of opinion that psychically inclined children do see images in patterns and other data, as well as staring into space or daydreaming. However, whether or not it was because I was an extremely frail and sickly child, I only ever saw them just before I was going to be very poorly and admitted to hospital, or when some trauma of one kind or another was going to befall my family. As I explained earlier the school I attended was for frail children with respiratory problems. This was a yellow-brick Baroque-style manor house set in acres of landscaped gardens and fields, and was donated by a wealthy nineteenth century merchant to be used for children with serious health problems. Underlea was an enchanted place where children could really live their dreams and get lost in the realms of imagination. I was sent there in 1953 when I was seven years old, and for a little boy who had grown up in a two up and two down terrace house in the centre of Liverpool, Underlea (which was in the suburbs of Liverpool) was like another world. Little wonder then that I was forever going missing and would hide away somewhere in the wood situated at the far end of the fields. It was there that I had my very first encounter with Nature Spirits; tiny creatures with gossamer-like wings and no bigger than the largest Dragonfly. However, they were not Dragonflies, as they were like tiny people with little faces. They would fly playfully about me in groups of five and sometimes more, and I would sit watching them enthralled as they danced on the fragrant air, before finally disappearing somewhere high up in the trees. I would continue to sit daydreaming on the decaying trunk of an old fallen tree, lost in my thoughts until the search party found me and ordered me to the headmaster's office for a scolding. Mr McMennamin was the headmaster and he always seemed to be in a bad mood. As he screamed at me with his broad Irish brogue, I could do nothing but stand helplessly rigid in front of him, my gaze locked upon his wide volatile eyes until all his anger had been spent. The colour now returning to his lined face, Mr McMennamin would shake his head and give me a look of sheer exasperation, before ordering me back to my classroom. I could never understand why he was always angry with me when all I had done was spend an hour in the wood by myself with my thoughts. Ever since I can recall I have been *clairaudient* (the ability to hear disembodied voices) and would sit in the wooded area of the school fields listening to the ethereal whisperings from another world, perhaps even from another time. Looking back I must have appeared extremely odd to the teachers let alone to the other children, and never, ever paid any attention to the lessons. Little wonder that I was well behind the other children my age and was put in the class with children 12 months my junior. At that age I did not care what class I was in, as I wasn't interested in anything but nature and religion. Although my mother was mediumistically inclined I must have been a big worry to her. She would always be there to meet me from the school bus every afternoon at 4.30pm prompt, and it would seem that I always had a story to tell her about some encounter or another. Although she always seemed to listen with great interest, looking back I'm certain now that she was just showing motherly interest in her son and most probably put most of my stories down to my huge imagination. Sometimes I would take my Angels' book of Promises with me to school, making quite certain that none of the other children even caught a glimpse of it. This was my secret book and something in which I would take great care to write on one page all the things I so badly wanted, and on the other the things I would promise to do in return. It was a simple process that always worked!

One can never be certain whether or not the things children say they have seen are embellishments of what really happened. Although I do have perfect recall of nearly everything I have experienced from the moment I came into this life, when I now look back to those days I sometimes question some of the things I then experienced. Nonetheless, some of the Angelic phenomena remain deeply engrained in my memory today, even though to speak of my experiences, even to my wife, brings some feelings of embarrassment.

ANGELS' FACES IN PATTERNS AND CLOUDS

Often when I prayed to my guardian Angel, something in the sky would attract my attention. Most children see faces in the clouds, but mine would always coincide with my prayer. Strange though it may sound the face I saw in the clouds would always be the same one, angelic and very gentle and would always be staring down at me. I know that this probably sounds a little ridiculous and you would be given for thinking that all children experience this sort of phenomenon; however, sometimes you have to be guided by intuition and faith, and I just *knew* that what I was seeing was somehow a manifestation of my very own Guardian Angel.

The parapsychological explanation for seeing faces and shapes in patterns is that it is a psychological phenomenon called Apophenia: seeing patterns or connections in random or meaningless data. One would think that at my age this phenomenon would no longer happen to me. On the contrary, it happens more consistently today than it did when I was a child; the only difference now is I know exactly what it is I am seeing and why I am seeing it.

I have never really been one for fanciful notions about angels. As far as I have always been concerned Angels are a fact of life and death, and whether you believe in them or not does not take away the fact that they are there either seen or unseen, watching us, and on many occasions manipulating circumstances to help us work our way through a difficult or traumatic period of our life. It is true that those who completely dismiss the existence of Angelic Beings simply have no need for them. Occasionally a rich man will dismiss Angels as being for the weak and the poor, but another will attribute his wealth, health and success to the fact that he was helped by Angels. The wealthy person who denies the existence of Angels is a bigger fool than he or she realises.

ANGELS IN PEOPLE

Anyone who has been in the very depths of despair and has not been able to see any end to their difficult plight, will perhaps understand exactly what I mean when I say that occasionally an angel comes along disguised as an ordinary person. I know many people use the word 'Angel' as a descriptive term and often use it when talking about someone who has done them a good turn. When we look at the good work some people do for those less fortunate than themselves, then one has to wonder what is it that drives that particular individual to do the good that they do, when many others simply turn away without a single caring thought. What is it that makes one person go out of his or her way to help someone in distress, and another person to look the other way? I know for certain that Angelic forces are always active, and that the Kingdom of Angels is quite able to influence the simplest of people to do good works here on earth. A cynic might say, 'but that's just the way some people are and nothing whatsoever to do with Angels!' Nonetheless, the sceptic can no more prove their point than I can prove mine, but when the sceptic finds him or herself in the depths of despair let us see what they think then. I would like to reiterate a line from a passage given earlier: *'Are the Divine recollections that slumber in your soul only to be awakened by the lance thrusts of grief?'* It is surely one of the most disappointing human failings that we only acknowledge the existence of Angels when we are in need of their help, and other times we deny their very existence.

I know that my mother believed totally in the existence of angels and even had a special prayer to call upon her own Guardian Angel. Although she was not particularly religious, when frosty patterns formed on the window in the winter time, she would always say, 'There you are, my Guardian Angel is watching over you.' Regardless of whether this was really true, my mother's words always gave me great comfort, especially when I was ill in bed.

NATURE SPIRITS AND FAIRIES AND THE PARTS THEY PLAY

I suppose the majority of those who believe in angels will most probably also believe in fairies and nature spirits, even though they may not have given it any thought whatsoever to how they are all connected. In fact, I often recall my mother's stern warning 'Never, ever say, you don't believe in Fairies! For every time you do the one that lives its life close to you will die!' At least, that's what my mother used to say, and I had no reason to doubt her.

They do say nymphs, fairies and other similar nature spirits will only go near children or adults who think pure thoughts and live simple and clean lives. Nymphs are allegedly minor goddesses or spirits in mythology and are attracted to areas of natural beauty, such as woodland, mountains and rivers, and other picturesque landscapes. And although they are traditionally portrayed as young beautiful women, many people believe that they are most definitely under the supervision of Angels. Just like angels they very rarely show themselves physically to anyone, but on the rare occasions they do they manifest as unusual light anomalies or other extraordinary phenomena. In fact, all things are controlled by an omnipotent, omnipresent power, and the Angels are the beings who minister over all. Nature Spirits and many other such creatures function within the Divine Laws of the *Great Cosmic Circle*. This so-called *Great Cosmic Circle* is comprised of a Hierarchy of Angelic Beings who mostly exist in the very subtle landscapes of the earth upon which we live and breathe. Legend has it that the *Great Cosmic Circle* is responsible for maintaining the equilibrium of the planet, and also for supervising Nature's Elementals as well as keeping a watchful eye on the ways in which the followers and lovers of nature conduct their worship. Those with a genuine interest in nature and who worship nature as a deity, providing they are true to their belief and have respect for the cause they follow, are very often guided and inspired by those within the *Great Cosmic Circle*. Those with an interest in Angels very often find it much easier to call upon *them* whilst sitting in the serenity of a picturesque landscape, such as in the countryside, in the shelter of woodland or by a running river. When one's imagination is extremely strong, these natural, picturesque landscapes are much more tangible and more likely to evoke images of Angelic beings of Light in the consciousness. There is very little doubt that the image-making faculty of the brain is an integral part of the whole process of Angel communication, and unless you are able to actually mentally create even the most rudimentary image of Angelic Beings, or for that matter any other such creatures, then you will most probably have some difficulty in having even a superficial encounter with them. It was once said to me in one of my later encounters with an Angelic Being of Light: *'Faith is believing without seeing, feeling without touching, and being happy and complete within yourself without receiving.'* This was said to me at a time when my faith was nearly non-existent and my imagination almost dead! It took me some time before the realisation of exactly what it meant and what *'they'* were trying to tell me actually dawned on me.

Nature Meditation is an extremely effective way of communing with nature and contacting Angelic Beings of Light. This is a very simple method of meditation and one which I have used for many years, particularly when I take a trip into the country.

For this method of meditation you will need two ear plugs and a blindfold, for reasons that will soon become clear. I would suggest that if you are asking for help with a particular problem that you take your *Angels' Book of Promises* along with you. By now I would assume that your book has been fully energised and empowered to the best of your ability. Remember, the book is personal to you and should therefore be treated at all times with the utmost respect.

Should you be fortunate enough to have a nice garden, then by all means take advantage of this. Otherwise, take a folding chair along with you to your chosen location, and sit quietly for a few moments holding your Angels' Book of Promises in your hands. Listen to the different sounds around you; birds singing in the trees, the rustling leaves in the wind. Make a mental note of as many sounds as you can; even far off sounds such as a dog barking, the sound of children playing; and when you feel quite ready close your eyes.

NATURE MEDITATION

- *Establish what it is you need from your Angels firmly in your mind, and dwell on it for several minutes. Try not to confuse them or the universe by allowing different things to pass through your consciousness. Make quite certain that you are ready to write it in your book.*

- *First of all write your request on the appropriate page, and then either underline it or draw a circle around it.*

- *Close your book and holding it comfortably in your hands, think about what you are going to do in return. In fact, what you are willing to do is just as important in the process of giving and receiving.*

- *Once you have decided, open your book again and enter this on the appropriate page. Underline it or draw a circle around it, just as you did previously. Close your book and hold it for a further few minutes.*

NEXT STEP:

- *Now, insert the earplugs into your ears, to eliminate all external sound; put on the blindfold, ensuring that no light can be seen at all. Remember, the object of this exercise is to establish contact with Nature Spirits, the Kingdom of Angel's ambassadors of nature.*

- *Sit quietly for at least ten minutes, imbibing the peaceful serenity of total silence. Be as perfectly still as possible, but be mindful of the book on your lap and the entries you have made in it.*

- *Now, allow your mind to move away from the book, and using the power of all your senses see what you can feel.*

- *Although you should neither see nor hear anything, your personal radar system should now be active and will immediately begin to scan the space around you. The longer you remain there the more you will begin to notice. At first sounds might appear muffled in the small space of your ear drum, and images may be nebulous as they pass through your consciousness.*

- *Be aware of everything that comes into your consciousness, and send out the mental command for the Nature Spirits to come close. Make it clear that your intentions are good and unselfish, and that you are seeking help from your Guardian Angels.*

- *Convey this message very clearly to the spirits of the woodland or to anyone who has taken an interest in your wellbeing.*

- *Make a mental note of everything you experience; even the slightest sensation, the most fleeting thought or indistinct sound is important in your mental analysis of the whole experiment.*

- *When you feel quite ready to conclude the exercise, remove the blindfold and earplugs, and then sit for a further five minutes collecting your thoughts.*

Even if you experienced nothing at all, it is an exercise that should be repeated several times. Remember, you are regarded as a stranger to the nymphs and other elementals, and will remain so until they are certain of your intentions. For this very reason you should not be impatient and expect results during the first experiment. Remember also, that it is an experiment and so try not to be too disappointed if you experience nothing. It is also important that you feel safe and comfortable during the exercise, and so it is something you should practise in an environment that is very familiar to you. Some people take along their dog for company; but only do this if it is not boisterous and you are certain it will sit quietly. Repeat it several times, always choosing the same spot each time.

WHEN ANGELS AND FAIRIES HAVE BEEN

It should also always be borne in mind that the whole object of the exercises given in this book is to make contact with Angelic Beings and to establish a strong relationship with them. Nature Spirits very often act as their messengers, and a peaceful land-loving relationship with angels brings about the same with Nature Spirits. Although it is a popular belief today that the calling card of Angels is a white feather, there are in fact many other more significant indications that they are around. Although a feather is quite tangible and can be kept as a keepsake, sometimes less tangible signs are experienced. For example, a waft of a very sweet, indescribable fragrance or Angel's faces in the patterns on the curtains or carpet, or even faces in the clouds, may occur, often in answer to your prayers. Another perhaps much rarer indication that an Angel has called is the phenomenon of 'Crossed Twigs' found either on the ground in the most unlikely of places, or on the surface of a piece of furniture, where you would not expect to find them. On very rare occasions the phenomenon involves two strands of straw, another indication that an Angel has called. On the conclusion of your Nature Meditation you may even find crossed twigs or straws at your feet, letting you know that you have been visited.

THE HISTORICAL MEANINGS OF NATURE SPIRITS

As gods and goddesses, nymphs and fauns appear in ancient mythologies, and among the medieval peoples, fairies are beings who preside over at birth and control the destiny of man. The word is actually from the Latin and is akin to fate. The English word 'fairy' originally meant 'enchanted', while the elf or spirit was designated by 'fay'. At an earlier date, however, the mistake was made of calling a fay a fairy, and the word fairy in the present context has been used ever since. In many of the older accounts of fairies there seems nothing in form, size or appearance to distinguish them from human beings, but they are known to possess supernatural knowledge and powers. However, in later accounts fairies were usually described as diminutive beings floating through the air. It was once said that fairies are only a few inches high, and that they are light and airy in form, enabling them to dance on a dewdrop. Fairies of one kind or another are found in every culture, and are believed by many to be the servants of angels on earth.

TOUCHED BY FAIRIES

Some cultures believe that if money was found the fairies had dropped it with benevolent intent. When Angels cannot influence wealth, they can instruct fairies to do so. If milk turns sour it is believed to be the work of fairies. Although patterns that form on a frosted window pane is believed to be a sign that an Angel has called, it is also a sign that fairies too have called to watch over you. The delicate gossamer webs often seen on a dewy morning are believed to be the fairies' washing spread out to dry. As is well known, many kinds of mushrooms grow in circles in remote places. A circle of these umbrella-like toadstools often springs up over night, and are called fairy rings, within which the fairies have danced. As there are Angelic Beings of Light to supervise different things, so are fairies appointed to take charge of different matters. Thus the elf is usually mischievous and sometimes known as 'the borrower', for reasons that they can steal personal items from us, only to return them to the most unlikely places. The sylph is a graceful, floating creature who lives in the air. It is believed that when the sylph brushes against your skin it immediately takes away your sadness and replaces it with feelings of joy. The gnome is grotesque and homely and is believed to live underground. When these creatures enter your life they bring security and sometimes wealth, and when they like you they remain in your environment forever. There are many different fairies that live in mines, and as long as they are respected and made welcome they will bring good luck and protect the miners. In Germany the cobald lives peacefully in the deepest mine shafts, and in Cornwall as long as the miner throws a piece of his pasty to the Cornish pisky it will protect and bring luck to him and his colleagues. The Irish banshee is a wrinkled, aristocratic old lady who appears under the windows of great houses and sings mournfully, warning the family of impending death. The Scottish brownies lurk about farm houses, and if made welcome and given food they will work hard while the farmer and his family sleep. Fairies allegedly inhabit a distinct realm in close proximity to the earth. Legend has it that the king of fairies is Oberon, as mentioned in an old French tale. Mab is the queen of fairies; a name which originates from the Welsh. Whether you believe in fairies or not, they are in every culture, and Celtic literature has innumerable stories concerning 'the little people' and how they help us with our struggles, traumas and hardships. They are believed to work very closely with the Angelic Kingdom, and it is further believed that when fairies take a particular liking to someone that person will be truly blessed in life.

One little known fact is that Angels and their graceful representatives in nature respond to certain human sounds. Chanting is an extremely effective way of creating a conducive environment for both angels and Nature Spirits, as well encouraging harmony in body, mind and spirit.

CHAPTER NINE

CHANTING WITH THE ANGELS

As I have said at the conclusion of the last chapter, chanting creates a more harmonious environment for angels and also has a vibratory effect upon the body, mind and spirit. Chanting forms the basis of certain methods of meditation, and when used correctly is good for the health. In the 1960s, physicist, the Maharishi Mahesh Yogi, was the innovator of a method of meditation he called Transcendental meditation, or TM as it became popularly known. I was fortunate to meet the Maharishi at a conference in the 1960s and really did learn a great deal from him. Transcendental Meditation involved chanting a word that was personal to the meditator, and was said to relieve stress and heighten the spiritual consciousness. More than this though chanting a mantra produces a resonance in the body affecting all the cells and holistically encouraging equilibrium of body mind and spirit. In fact, the concept of chanting has been used by many cultures for thousands of years and has always been an extremely effective way of precipitating the consciousness into transcendental states of awareness.

CHANTING WITH ANGELS IN MIND
When mantras are used in relation to establishing a relationship with Angels, certain sounds may be effectively used. Although these can take many forms, the ones I have always used produce remarkable results and have a particular resonance with that part of the brain responsible for communication with the supersensual side of the universe. These can also be used to gain access to that particular dimension of the supersensual universe, inhabited by members of the celestial community.

If need be the mantras can be easily modified to suit you. To begin with, each mantra affects its corresponding part of the anatomy, and when chanted in sequential order, the overall vibratory sound of the body is increased, thus producing a powerful resonance with the universal pulse.

PROCESS OF INCREASING THE VIBRATORY RATE OF THE BODY

MMEE – *The word should be chanted as it is written. This produces an amazing effect upon the pituitary and pineal glands, and encourages an increase in the electromagnetic waves emanating from the pineal gland. To use the mantra, inhale a complete breath, and then chant the word until all the breath has been fully exhaled. Repeat the process four times before moving on to the next.*

EA - *Ea should be sounded as in the word 'feather'. This mantra affects the throat area, and particularly affects the thyroid. As previously explained, inhale a complete breath, and then sound the word until all the breath has been fully expelled. Repeat this four times before moving on to the next sound.*

AAA - *Aaa should be sounded like the word 'Grass', following the same procedure as previously shown. This particular mantra affects the upper respiratory area of the body.*

OU-O - *Ou-o should be sounded as in the word, 'water', with the same procedure as given with the previous mantras. The vibrations with this sound affect the middle area of the chest.*

Ooo - *Ooo should be sounded like the word 'Home', again with the same breathing procedure as previously shown. This word has a remarkable effect upon the lower part of the lungs, the heart, stomach and liver.*

EUR - *Eur should be sounded as in the French word 'Fleur', and chanted in the same way as the previously given words. The vibratory sounds of this word affect the diaphragm and surrounding area.*

U-EE – *U-ee should be sounded as in 'You-ee', and allowed to resonate until the breath has been fully expelled. The vibratory sounds of this word affect the gonads of the male and female reproductive system.*

As I have previously explained, for maximum results, each word should be chanted no more than four times in sequential order each session. Even though positive results will be achieved in a very short time, you should persist with the practice for at least a month, longer if you feel comfortable. The different sounds increase the vibratory rate of the subtle anatomy and encourage a greater frequency of the movement of the individual chakras – the vortices of energy that lie along the surface of the etheric tract in the spinal column. The chakra system's responsibility is to encourage balance and equilibrium of body, mind and spirit, thus ensuring that the health of the body is maintained. Although just words, mantras have an almost magical effect upon the body, by causing a dramatic increase in its vibratory rate. After the chanting has been concluded, ten minutes or so should be spent using your preferred method of angel meditation. Your Angels' Book of Promises should always be integrated into any exercise you use, particularly that the whole object of the book is to establish a relationship with the Kingdom of Angels. Remember the biblical precept, '*Ask and it shall be given.*'

As I have already said, use the mantras sequentially for approximately a month or as long as it takes for you to really feel the benefit. You will recognise the moment when you are ready to move on to the next part of the exercise. You will experience an 'inner-glow' and an overwhelming feeling of elation that really cannot be described with words.

Once full benefits have been achieved with the above mantras, the sequence should only be chanted when you feel in need of an overhaul.

The following mantra increases the vibratory rate of the throat and brow chakras specifically, and should precede any angel ritual. Practised for a period of ten minutes before your meditation ritual, the mantra will increase the levels of energy in the whole ritualistic exercise. Before the chanting commences, spend a few minutes regulating your breathing, ensuring that the inhalations and exhalations of breath are evenly spaced. Inhale a complete breath, and then begin chanting the mantra on the exhalation of the breath. When the breath has been fully expelled, inhale a complete breath and then repeat the whole process. Before beginning the chanting process, it is a good idea if you read the mantra a few times to familiarise yourself with it. Ideally, for maximum effect, you should learn it first by rote.

PAA-PARA-PAA-EEM-MAA-PAA-PARA-PAA-EEM-MAA

Simply repeat the chanting of the above, whilst focusing the attention on your forehead. Initially it is not necessary to close your eyes, but once the mantra has been fully fixed in your memory, the eyes should then be closed. As well as encouraging an increase in the energy of the throat and brow chakras, *PAA-PARA-PAA-EEM-MAA-PAA-PARA-PAA-EEM-MAA* raises the vibratory tones of the body. In so doing it helps to establish 'contact' with the Celestial Beings closest to you, just like tuning a radio into your favourite station. The mantra can also be used as a means of raising healing vibrations when healing is needed, either for yourself or for someone else. Before chanting it all that you need to do is send out the mental command that healing is required. If it is your intention to establish a relationship with your angelic guardians primarily for healing, it is a good idea to create an Angels' book specifically with this in mind. The layout of an Angels' Healing Book is quite straightforward. Simply write on one page the name of the person for whom healing is requested, and on the other page what he or she is suffering from. As with any of the angels' books you create, it is important that nobody other than yourself sees or touches it. The book must be regarded as 'sacred' and a direct link to the Kingdom of Angels. This contributes to its empowerment and encourages greater healing to be created.

KODOISH MANTRA

Finally, one of the most powerful mantras is *KODOISH, KODOISH, KODOISH, ADONAI, TSBEYOTH.* This Hebrew mantra affects all the cells in the body and is believed to resonate with the number 999, the highest frequency on earth. The mantra means Holy, Holy, Holy, Lord of Hosts and creates a screen of Divine Energy, allowing the consciousness to be raised sufficiently to cause unification with God and the Kingdom of Angels. When used at least once a day, the mantra encourages activation of every subatomic particle and affords protection on all levels of consciousness.

HERE'S WHAT TO DO

- *Before you begin familiarise yourself with the mantra by reading it several times. If possible learn it by rote so that it is firmly fixed in your mind.*

- *It helps if you have a small bell at hand to ring occasionally. Apart from its pleasant sound, the chime also helps you to chant at the correct tone. Burning some pleasant incense also helps to set the mood.*

- *Sit quietly with your Angels' Book of Promises in your hands. Breathe rhythmically for a few moments until the rhythm is fully established in your mind and your mind is sufficiently quiet to begin chanting.*

- *Ring the bell to begin the chanting, and then ring it every few moments, or when you feel a need.*

- *Begin chanting out loud, repeating the mantra over and over for several minutes, longer if you like. KODOISH, KODOISH, KODOISH, ADONAI, TSBEYOTH. KODOISH, KODOISH, KODOISH, ADONAI, TSBEYOTH, and so on. I would suggest maintaining the chanting for as long as you can, and on its conclusion sit quietly for a further five minutes to obtain maximum benefits.*

I have found the Kodoish Mantra to be an excellent 'pick-me-up' whenever I am feeling out of sorts or even a little depressed. It produces a powerful 'washing' effect over the whole body, and affords the chanter protection from negative forces as well as encouraging an increase in vitality. You may then feel a need to write something in your Angels' Book of Promises.

It is also an extremely powerful mantra for anyone who may be suffering from the pains of bereavement and really does bring instant relief.

As there are angels to deliver our loved ones safely to the next world, so are there angels to bring comfort to those who have been left behind. The Angels' Book of Promises is also a healing balm for those in need of comfort at this very sad time. On the conclusion of chanting the Kodoish mantra it is a good idea to sit quietly with your eyes closed, allowing your mind to imbibe the therapeutic vibrations.

SILENCE

There are suggestions in the psychology of meditation that there are two specific types of *silence*; a *Passive* silence, and an *Active* silence. Passive silence is the silence of non-existence, of sleep and of death, and the silence over which we have no control. Active silence is that of meditation or of simply stilling the lips in contemplative thought. Mystics of old suggest that 'silence is a supernatural burden whose inexplicable weight brings dread to the mightiest soul. And in crowds those who fear it seek isolation and to drive away the invisible enemy of silence. For some have no silence at all, and they destroy all the silence about them. In fact, these are the only creatures who pass through life unperceived, and to them it is not given to cross that zone of revelation, that beautiful zone of firm and faithful light, wherein the angels dwell.'

CHAPTER TEN

ANGELS' SACRED MEMORIAL SPACE

Death is perhaps the one single thing we all have in common, and a process we cannot avoid. It matters not how wealthy you are, when your time is up there's absolutely nothing whatsoever you can do to prevent dying. Of course wealth can very often make the end of your life more comfortable, and even get you the very best in private medical care, but the rest is entirely in the hands of God, as they say! The other painful situation that we are forced to face in life is actually losing someone we love. This is very often an unbearable pain and one that is so difficult to ease. Although I have been a professional medium for thirty years it is only on rare occasions that I would suggest consulting a medium to ease the pain of bereavement. Very often (depending on the medium) this can cause more anguish and do more harm than good. A few years ago now a young woman phoned my office to make an appointment for her father. Although she never said what her father was looking for, she did explain that he was elderly and that he had never seen a medium before.

The appointment was made for 3pm the following afternoon, but by 4pm the man had still not arrived. My wife looked through the window and noticed an elderly man standing nervously on the opposite side of the road watching the office intently. It was obviously the man I had been waiting for, so my wife went over to talk to him. When he walked into my office I could feel the immense pressure emanating from him and then he broke down and explained what was wrong. He had been married to his wife for 50 years until she died suddenly of a heart attack. I did not think it was morally right to give him a private consultation so soon after his wife had died, so I just sat listening to him for over an hour, letting him get it out of his system. He could not quite grasp where his wife had gone and went on to explain that he would wander round the streets of Liverpool in the middle of the night looking for her. He was understandably totally distraught and had even contemplated ending his own life so that he could be with her. He was a simple man, in the nicest possible way, and so there was absolutely no use explaining the nature of the spirit world to him. However, there was something that would help him, and he would not even have to leave the safety of his own home. The Angels' Sacred Memorial Space is something that has helped thousands of people to come to terms with their loss. It is an extremely simple process that apart from a little preparation requires virtually no effort at all.

ANGELS' SACRED MEMORIAL SPACE

Whether you have a belief in an afterlife or not, your loved ones never die – they simply move to a different place in your heart. There is an extremely effective way of easing the pain of such a loss, and this involves creating a Sacred Space with a difference. Although this has nothing whatsoever to do with faith or belief in a particular religion, the *Angels' Sacred Memorial Space* is a corner of the house or garden where you can be alone with your thoughts and feel the closeness of your loved one.

All that you need is a laminated photograph of yourself with the person for whom you are grieving, some small pieces of Amethyst and Rose Quartz crystals, a vase for flowers, and also an Angels' Book of Promises. Although your Sacred Space can be created in your home, it is much more atmospheric in the garden, weather permitting. If you do choose to create it in the garden it is a good idea to erect a small shelter in which to sit when it is raining.

THE PROCESS

- *Select a quiet corner in the garden and place either a bench or seat strategically in position.*

- *Secure the laminated photograph in the appropriate place and surround it with the small crystals, in no particular order. Make it as decorative as you want, and then place the vase with flowers or even a single flower in front of the photograph.*

- *You can also place other sentimental mementos in your Sacred Space; in fact, anything that will help to remind you of your loved one.*

- *Whenever you feel that the pain is too great to bear, take you Angels' Book of Promises to your Sacred Space and sit there quietly, holding your book gently in your hands.*

- *For the purpose of this exercise it might be a good idea if you were to stick a few photographs strategically in your book, and write next to them your private thoughts, as well as what you would like from the Angels. On the opposite page enter exactly what you are going to do in return. It might be a good idea to write how you intend to cope with your grief, as well as how you feel about the person you have lost. You may initially think that this is all a waste of time, but persistence will bring its rewards and most probably sooner than you think.*

- *The more you use your Angels' Sacred Memorial Space, the more powerful and effective it will become in bringing you peace and serenity.*

- *Instead of withdrawing to your room, or mentally and emotionally turning off when you are feeling sad, get into the habit of taking your grief into your Angels' Sacred Memorial Space. Only by using your Sacred Space in this way will you empower it with the required healing balm. The psychological effects of this are very quick and therapeutic, and you should come to feel your loved one there with you. If you can understand that that there are no alternating periods of night or day in the spirit world, and that very often your loved one needs something upon which to focus, then you should understand that when your emotions are all over the place, then so is your loved one. If you get into the habit of entering your Sacred Space when you are feeling tearful and unhappy, they will know that they are to be there too. As well as that you will feel comforted by the whole healing process, and will feel as though you have been visited by an angel.*

As there are Angels to help and guide us in our aspirations, so too are there Angels to comfort us in times of great sorrow and unhappiness. Being mindful of and believing in Angelic Beings of Light helps to create a portal through which they can enter our lives. To outwardly deny the existence of Angelic Beings of Light is to prevent them from gaining access into our lives. If you use your Angels' Book of Promises whilst sitting quietly in your Sacred memorial Space, you can rest assured that you will be visited by the angels who have been charged with your care.

As well as the previously explained use of the Angels' Book of Promises, the psychological effect also needs to be considered. Where grief is concerned making entries in the book is a healing process in itself and encourages the release of a great deal of sadness, emotional distress and anger, when it is felt that is. The whole process can either be a religious or non-religious exercise, depending on your belief or lack of it, whichever the case may be.

Your Angels' Book of Promises will become even more sacred, stronger and much more effective with use.

ANGEL EXPERIMENT IN CONSCIOUSNESS

Whenever I am conducting a meditation workshop I always like to make it very clear to those participating that what meditation technique suits one person may not necessarily suit another. When dealing with altered states of consciousness and the expansion of awareness, the way in which people are affected by meditation varies from person to person. Understanding this I always create a meditation method specifically for the individual, or at least help him or her to modify the technique that they feel most comfortable with. I have said elsewhere in this book that meditation is in fact the highest form of prayer, and is the means by which all great minds seek to attain the highest point of light. Technically speaking meditation is a means with which to focus the attention on one particularly thing or idea to the exclusion of everything else. This is far easier said than done considering that the mind tends to wander from one thing to another, rather like a butterfly flitting from flower to flower. Ideally, emptying the mind completely would bring about the desired results, but as any practitioner of meditation will affirm emptying the mind completely is impossible. The mind is an amazing computer logged-in at all times to the cyber space of human consciousness, and so all that one can learn to do is to master it and bring it under control. Once the fundamental principles of meditation have been fully understood, you will then be able to explore this mental internet with greater ease, to thus navigate your way through the internal planes of consciousness, destination anywhere you choose.

Meditation is also an ideal tool with which to encourage the unification of consciousness with the Celestial planes. Once you have mastered a suitable meditation technique you should have no problem at all in having a transcendental experience, (albeit for a brief moment,) in the *light* of Celestial consciousness.

SELF-CREATED DEMONS

Meditation helped me to deal with many of my self-created demons during the darkest periods of my life, and eventually helped to awaken in me aspects of my *being* I never knew existed. Working on the premise that you are what you *think*, I had spent many years thinking in the darkness and had established in my life a dense environment peopled by thought demons to which none other than myself had given life. This may sound very much from the pages of a 'Stephen King' book, but it is really the only way I can explain it to you. The point I am trying to make is that it does not matter how low you have fallen, or how many demons you have created in your life, the angels are always close by and ready to help. This particular meditation is different from the others previously given in this book, inasmuch as it is simply an exercise in visualisation, and a gentle and effective way of expanding the consciousness. It is also an extremely effective mental process for those who find meditation itself laboriously difficult.

A CREATIVE JOURNEY TO THE KINGDOM OF ANGELS

The image-making faculty of the brain is an incredible organ that can lead you anywhere. Once you have truly accepted the existence of Angels, and you have gone through the process of creating your own Sacred Space, burn some pleasant incense and put on an appropriate piece of music. These will encourage the consciousness on the beautiful, mind-expanding journey to the Celestial planes.. Before you begin it is a good idea to read through the exercise several times so that you know exactly what you are doing and will not have to keep referring to the text.

- *Sit on a straight backed chair in the usual position, making certain that your chest, neck and head are as nearly in a straight line as possible, with your shoulders thrown slightly back and your hands resting comfortably on your lap.*

- *As you have done previously breathe rhythmically until the rhythm is fully established, ensuring that the inhalations and exhalations are evenly spaced. When you feel quite relaxed you can then begin the journey.*

- *In your mind create large ornate golden gates, through which you can see a long driveway leading to an incredible mansion set in acres of geometrically landscaped gardens. Notice that everything seems to shimmer and pulsate with its own self-created light.*

- *Remain there for a few moments staring in awe through the golden gates at the mansion. The magnificent edifice seems to shimmer rather like mother-of-pearl, and radiates an iridescent light. Everything is bright and very surreal, almost as though you are dreaming.*

- *The ornate golden gates slowly open and you pass through them and begin to meander along the driveway towards the manor house in the distance. Feel yourself moving slightly quicker now, propelled by an unusual force with your feet not even touching the ground.*

- *Within moments you find yourself at the bottom of seven stone steps leading up to the large ornately carved wooden doors, which open of their own accord.*

- *As you slowly ascend the seven stone steps they each light up in a colour of the spectrum. As your feet touch each step mentally see the colours, Red, Orange, Yellow, Green, Blue, Indigo and Violet. Feel the colours as well as see them, and allow their individual energies to pass through you.*

INSIDE THE MANSION

- *Now enter the spacious hallway and see light cascading down through a glass domed ceiling above, breaking into a myriad of different shades of colours as it hits the mosaic marble floor, itself a source of pulsating light.*

- *You have the overwhelming feeling that you are in a place that transcends the confines of physical experience, and a place which is the source of life itself.*

CLIMBING THE STAIRCASE

- *In front of you there is a broad staircase that leads up to a large stained glass window at the top before turning to disappear out of sight. Climb the stairs slowly, mindful of each step taking you to a different aspect of your mind, and nearer to your Guardian Angel.*

- *Feel a rush of expectation as you slowly ascend the staircase, mentally scanning your surroundings as you move higher and higher.*

- *You reach the top of the staircase and stand in front of the stained glass window. You notice the different coloured glass has been meticulously fashioned in the image of an angel, reminding you of the reason you are there.*

- *Move round to your left and continue to the very top of the staircase, and there you see a long corridor with five doors along one side, and five doors along the other.*

SELECTING A DOOR

- *Select a door, and follow the corridor until you reach the one you have chosen. Open it and enter the room.*

- *Allow your imagination to create the room. As long as there is a large window overlooking the beautiful gardens, you can make the room look anyway you want.*

- *It is important that you feel comfortable in the room, and should there be anything whatsoever that you find unpleasant, then you must change it.*

- *Look out of the window down to the gardens below, making a mental note of everything you can see.*

GUARDIAN ANGEL

- *You suddenly hear the door open behind you, and when you turn round there is a statuesque figure standing there attired in a white shimmering gown. You know instinctively that this is your Guardian Angel and you are immediately overwhelmed with the feeling that you already know him. This puts you at ease.*

- *He proffers both hands, and when you reach out to take them you are immediately infused with a powerful force that passes through you like a surge of electricity. It is extremely important to the whole experience that you feel energised and your whole body aglow with vitality and colour.*

- *Although no words are exchanged you seem to know exactly what he is thinking. At this point it is important that you let him know exactly what you are seeking to achieve in your life and how you would like him to help you.*

- *Spend a few moments looking at him and memorising everything you can about the way he looks. Make a mental note of his features; the colour of his eyes, the shape of his face and nose. His hair is long and wavy and hangs loosely about his shoulders. Make sure the image of your Guardian Angel is fixed firmly in your mind, and when you feel ready, bid him farewell and then move from the room.*

RETRACING YOUR STEPS TO THE FRONT DOOR

- *Close the door behind you, and then move slowly back along the corridor towards the staircase, following the same route back down the stairs, under the stained glass window with the image of the angel, then turn to your right to slowly descend the stairs. Take your time descending the stairs, taking care to make a mental note of everything around you.*

- *Reach the bottom of the broad staircase and stand on the mosaic marble floor and look up at the light cascading down from the glass domed ceiling above. Watch how the intense light hits the floor before breaking into a beautiful kaleidoscope of many colours. Feel energised by the colourful display, before turning to face the front door.*

- *Move slowly towards the front door (which is open) and pass through it onto the stone steps. As you ascend the steps the colours of the spectrum light up in reverse order. Violet, Indigo, Blue, Green, Yellow, Orange and finally Red. Remain on the red step for a few moments, feeling its powerful energy filling your whole body.*

- *Now, feel some invisible force carrying you along the driveway, and when you reach the ornate golden gates stand for a moments looking back at the almost surreal edifice, shimmering like mother-of-pearl in its own self-created light.*

- *Pass through the golden gates and watch as they slowly close behind you. Stand there for a few moments imbibing the peace and tranquillity.*

- *Breathe in very slowly, and as you breathe out dissolve it all from your mind, and when you are quite ready open your eyes.*

THE FINAL ANALYSIS

Do not dismiss this experiment in visualisation because of its simplicity! In fact, the whole visualisation experience is a psychological experiment and one which is designed to take you on a journey of self-discovery. The ornate golden gates symbolise closing your eyes on the first approach to meditation. The driveway represents your mental approach to the first stages of creating the imagery. Entering the mansion represents the raising of your consciousness, and the broad staircase leading to the upstairs corridor represents the inner states of mind. When you entered the room of your choice you consciously accessed the deepest part of your mind whereby your consciousness transcended physical experience. For this reason it is vitally important to always allow your imagination to create the correct ambience, and should this not be to your liking, then the next step is for you to change it until you feel comfortable.

This is just one of the many effective visualisation exercises to help you make contact with your Guardian Angel. The image-making faculty plays an integral part in processing the information coming into your consciousness from the supersensual universe, and although you may dismiss your encounter as little more than 'Imagination', all things are possible once the image-making faculty has been fully exercised.

By now you should understand the fundamental principles of the Angels' Book of Promises and how it can work for you. Its simplicity is what makes it powerful and effective, and once you get into the habit of using it whenever you need it, contact with your book alone will encourage the release of a powerful force that will give your solace when you need it most. Frequent use of your Angels' Book of Promises ritualistically also encourages the release of endorphins (the body's natural morphine-like substances) that help promote feelings of elation and well-being.

THE PHENOMENON OF THOUGHT FORMS

It may come as an extremely shocking surprise to many people but we really are the architects of our own destiny by the way we think. Our thoughts always crystallise into habit, and habit eventually solidifies into circumstance. We are always willing to change our circumstances but rarely willing to change ourselves and the way we think. And so, in accordance with the Universal Law of Attraction until we make radical changes to the way we *think*, our circumstances will always remain the same. In fact, we are constantly peopling our own private portion of space by the way we think, and the way we think is exactly the way we are. This law is as effective in the mental and moral worlds as much as it is in the physical world. Generally speaking a so-called *thought form* is a concentration of energy that assumes the shape or form that we ourselves desire. A thought form can assume the shape of the demon in your worst nightmare, or take on the guise of your most beautiful dream. The things we persistently fear and the things we consistently wish for in time become external images embedded in the self-created environment of our own mind. If you dwell upon something, be it good or bad, for any length of time, nature will always conspire to lead you into a position whereby you be able to bring about the gratification of your passions and desires. The universal Laws of Attraction are never wrong. In fact, this law is in constant operation all through our lives. We reap what we sow, not as a punishment for what we have done wrong, but because the effect must always follow the cause. Even accident is the result of ignorance and is due to the working of laws whose presence was overlooked or unknown. In the mental as much as the moral worlds, results can be foreseen, planned for, calculated on. The universe will never betray us, we are in fact betrayed by our own blindness – our own ignorance. Theology teaches that we are punished for our sins, but the higher teachings of the universe inform us that we are punished by our mistakes and not for them. An understanding of these laws is a prerequisite for working with the Kingdom of Angels; and once your relationship with the angels working closely with you has been well and truly established, so the necessary transformation to your thinking will fully come about.

SPIRIT GUIDES AND ANGELS

Although I fully accept the existence of Spirit Guides, I have come to see them as the servants of angels whose job it is very often to mediate between the Angelic Kingdom of light and this world of earth, sky and human habitations. Occasionally, however, spirit guides can be no more than the manifestations of thought forms, self-created out of the desire and need to be looked after by 'something' not of this world. If this process works with spirit guides there is no doubt that it can also work with angels.

For example, should you strongly believe that you have a powerful Spirit Guide who was once a great Egyptian King, the notion is gradually absorbed by the subconscious mind to eventually take on the form of the suggested noble entity. The image you yourself have created is then released with sufficient intelligence to allow it to eventually manifest as a living entity ready to do your bidding. This thought form can of course be seen by clairvoyants who merely empower it even more by describing it to you.

PRAYING TO SAINTS AND ANGELS

A devout catholic who prays regularly to a specific saint or angel will very often unknowingly create a thought form in the image of that saint and angel. Although a perfectly replicated image, the thought form only possesses the power that the person praying expects of it. Even so, the thought form is still able to fulfil certain obligations and may in some cases perform the function somewhat like the Genie in the Magic Lamp.

THE THOUGHT FORMS OF A NATION

On a much larger scale thought forms can permeate a nation stricken by famine or war, hovering like clouds in the atmosphere, and are energised by both the anguish and the prayers of those who live there. The prayers of a religiously devout impoverished nation collectively manifest as thoughts forms that float in the psychic space, rather like clouds in the atmosphere. These influence the minds of all those who come within the confines of their radiations, either for good or for ill, depending on the individual minds that created them. Should the majority of those in a nation stricken by famine or war harbour no particular religious beliefs, then the heavy emotions with which the thought forms have been initially created merely suffice to perpetuate the distress and anguish experienced by all those who dwell there. The various waves of thought we release during our lifetime, attract and are thus attracted by thoughts of a similar nature. They form thought strata in the psychic space in very much the same way that clouds fall into groups in the atmosphere. This does not mean that each stratum of thought occupies a portion of space to the exclusion of all other thought clouds; on the contrary, the particles of thought forming the clouds are of different degrees of vibration, and so the same space may be filled with thought matter of a thousand kinds, passing freely and interpenetrating each other without interference. In fact, each individual draws to himself thoughts corresponding with those produced by his own mind; and he is in turn influenced by those thoughts. Giving a much clearer understanding to the precept, 'You are what you think!' It is an axiom of physics that no two bodies of matter can occupy the same space at the same time; but millions of vibrations can exist in the one space at the same time, interpenetrating each other without interference. This is the nature of the universe and the way in which one dimension overlaps and inter-penetrates the other, each rising in a vibratory ascending scale, from those which touch and blend with the highest planes of the physical world, to those which gradually merge with the lowest spheres of the so-called 'Astral World.'

PRAYER

Prayer is an extremely effective mantra and an efficient way of releasing thought vibrations into the universe.

Prayer is in fact the most effective way of connecting with the divine power and facilitating the help of any thought forms that might have collected in your subtle environment. Angels are quite capable of manipulating positive thought forms and infusing them with even more power to affect changes or create healing in a nation stricken by war or famine. Occasionally a person's prayers and strong belief in Celestial beings will create the very image of the angel to whom he or she is praying. Although *thought forms* created in the images of saints or Angels are self-created *beings*, they will very often possess sufficient power to answer a prayer and bring whatever it is the individual who created them is asking for. In fact, thought forms can be so immensely powerful that there have been cases where their images have been captured on film and even photographed by an ordinary digital camera. Simply by focusing the mind for any length of time on the image of a Celestial being is all that is required to create a sufficiently powerful entity to watch over and guide you through the difficulties of your life. Many people who pray to particular Saints or exalted beings are helped by the images they themselves have created. These images cosmically represent the one who is the object of the prayer. Let us not forget that prayer is an extremely powerful tool, whether uttered quietly or mentally recited. It resounds through the universe to that place where all angels reside. Prayers are always answered and should therefore never be underestimated. A particular prayer, used on a regular basis, can very often create such powerful energies as to 'connect' the individual's mind to the Great 'Celestial Light', a phenomenon that is capable of causing miracles to happen. Although a person's faith plays an integral part in the actual manifestation of miracles, there are odd occasions when they can occur in the life of a devout atheist.

ANGEL APPEARS TO A PRISONER

One such manifestation was in the life of persistent offender, Les Weaveson. The thirty-five year old man had resigned himself to a life of crime and had just been sentenced to 18 months for the burglary of a warehouse. It was a cold and blustery November night and Les was lying on his bed in the darkened cell, when his attention was caught by a very bright light in the corner. He sat bolt upright and swung his legs over the side of the bed, but before he could go to investigate the unusual light anomaly, it metamorphosed into a lady dressed in a white shimmering gown. Although Les had never believed in anything of a super-natural nature, he was transfixed by the apparition and unable to move. He felt paralysed and all he could do was watch the angelic looking lady as she smiled. Although no words transpired between the two, her thoughts were telepathically transmitted to him. Les Weaveson never divulged what his celestial visitor had said to him, but whatever it was his life changed from that moment on. An appeal made by his solicitor was successful, and he was released on two years parole. Today Les is in full time employment working with young offenders, and is also happily married with a daughter. Whatever his Celestial Visitor said to him no one will ever know. But, one thing is certain, her visit changed his life forever. Angelic intervention occasionally occurs when a persistent offender shows promise and possesses a spark of decency. When an angel touches your life, the effects are very often long-reaching, as in the case of Les Weaveson who really did experience a huge spiritual transformation.

I have found in my thirty years of studying metaphysical and esoteric traditions that the more I learn about angels, the less I know. However, I have learnt that so-called Spirit Guides are much more than the disembodied beings who look after and inspire mediums and others undertaking some form of spiritual work. Spirit Guides are possibly closer to the Angelic Kingdom than we mortals realise.

CHAPTER THIRTEEN

SPIRIT GUIDES AND ANGELS

Sceptics nearly always use so-called 'Spirit Guides' as the focus of ridicule and humour, and few very rarely accept that angels themselves exist at all. This is why I have never really spoken out about my interest in angels and the phenomenon of Spirit Guides until now, for fear that I too would be ridiculed. I began to make a detailed study of the phenomenon of angels and human experience thirty years ago now, and my conclusions have led me to understand these Celestial Beings more fully. My own relationship with Tall Pine, has always been extremely strong, and although I never really speak about him during radio or television interviews,(unless I am asked,) he has always been an integral part of my life. From the very beginning of my recovery from a 12 year drug addiction Tall Pine (TP as he is affectionately still known) was there watching over and guiding me through that horrific period of my life. At this point in my life I really did not know how to control my psychic abilities and it seemed that *they* were in fact controlling me. Because of my emotional and psychological states I was obviously transmitting the wrong mental signal to the universe, and whatever forces I was sending out ultimately came back two-fold to me. I began to attract discarnates of a low order of mind, who seemingly saw me as some sort of kindred spirit and someone with whom there was a strong affinity. Young people who had died from drug overdoses would come to me in the dead of night, obviously in search of help and guidance. As I could not even help myself, how could I help anyone else?.

As I have mentioned in a previous chapter Tall Pine is a spirit guide and someone who has been with me since I was a child.

Although he had always been there in the periphery of my life, contact with him during my drug-crazed years was somewhat rare. However, now his appearances became more and more frequent and I would get great comfort from seeing him standing there in the shadows of my bedroom, silently watching me through the night. Some nights my room would be filled with all different kinds of light anomalies (today fashionably called 'orbs') or spirit lights, gyrating round in the darkness, as though in an attempt to entertain me. During this period of my life I once again felt Tall Pine very close to me, but it wasn't until the Elders (as they were introduced to me) really became involved in my life that I began to see clearly the light at the end of the proverbial tunnel. The Elders had been an integral part of my life since I was a child, and always appeared to me attired in long monsastic robes of shimmering light, just like my other angelic visitors. Although at that time because of total lack of spiritual understanding the teachings they began to impart to me were academic, they did stimulate in me an overwhelming desire and thirst for knowledge. I soon began to really understand the concept of spirit guides and guardian angels, and it was explained to me that the persona they present to us is primarily for the purpose of identification. Unfortunately, as I have already explained these 'spiritual warriors' are rarely taken seriously; an attitude that has always greatly frustrated and angered me. As Tall Pine had been with me since I was a child I knew full well that he was not a thought form, but was as tangible as everyone else around me. Even the most sceptical, non-religious individual is watched over by a spirit guide or guardian angel. A spirit guide is usually a highly evolved disembodied spirit who serves as a bridge of communication between this world and the next.

In Shamanism spirit guides manifest as animals and are called Totems. The tribal communities of North America chose animals that they believed represented the actual spirit of their character and personality. The belief was that in choosing a particular animal the strength, power or wisdom of that animal would be passed on to them. Sometimes a Totem would be a natural phenomenon, such as an erupting volcano or even a flash of lightning; it could even be a physical feature or even a hand-made artefact. This belief may account for the reason why spirit guides nearly always appear to be Native American. Shamanism is a primitive religion built about the magical and prophetic powers of a priest or medicine man. Shamanism is common among Ural-Altaic peoples of northern Europe and north western Asia whose cultural development is not far advanced. These include the Eskimos, Mongolians, Kirghiz and Tungus. The religion of most American Indian tribes is related to Shamanism in one form or another.

The Shaman, or medicine man, is a priest believed to have the power to influence through spells and incantations the many spirits, both good and evil, that are thought to preside over man's fortunes. The beating of drums is very often an integral part of the Shaman's ritual. His position is usually hereditary, and he is believed to be possessed and directed by the ghost of a dead ancestor.

A spirit guide is often referred to as the ambassador for the guardian angel who serves as the direct messenger of God. Although the majority of people do have many so-called spirit guides, each one responsible for the individual's different spiritual attributes, it is the so-called 'Gatekeeper' who lives his or her life in close proximity to the person with whom there is an affinity. The Gatekeeper is the spiritual disembodied energy that protects the individual from harmful people or situations, and stands guard over the 'Gate of Consciousness.' It has been suggested that a Spirit Guide may also be a facet of our own inner or higher self. As we evolve spiritually another facet manifests in our spiritual consciousness. Although Spirit Guides nearly always remain with us only a short while, perhaps to supervise our spiritual development until it reaches a certain degree, the Gatekeeper has most probably been with us long before we were born into this life, and will no doubt remain with us into the next life. In many ways can the Gatekeeper be described as an integral part of our soul group, ensuring that we take the right decisions in life and always follow the correct route. It is a fallacy that spirit guides lead us down the easiest road. Nothing would be gained by them or us in following an easy, straightforward path. Life is the constant accumulation of knowledge, the storing up of the results of experience; we reap what we sow not as a punishment for what we have done wrong, but because the effect must always follow the cause. This is the Law of Karma which is in constant operation all through our lives. As we evolve spiritually so do our spirit guides.

Supervising all those Spirit Guides who choose to guide us through life are the Angelic Beings of Light, a Supreme Hierarchy of Celestial beings who are always in the periphery of our life, watching and waiting for the invitation to call. The Angels' Book of Promises is a highly effective way of controlling the events of our life, at a spiritual as well as a physical level. The Angels' Book of Promises is not just a record of the requests you are making to your guiding Angels, but is also a tangible and visual affirmation to the universe. Making entries in the book is confirmation of your faith and belief in the whole celestial process. Unlike angelic beings Spirit Guides are able to live quite easily in the lower vibratory realms of the earth, very close to those they are guiding. They can inspire, control and entrance a person living in the corporeal world, and just like angels they have the power to transfigure over people and everyday objects, and even change form and cause things to move telekinetically. Because the powers of a Spirit Guide often transcend the parameters of science, the phenomena they produce are often attributed to Angels.

Whilst the majority of spirit guides are quite real, as I have previously stated, a small minority are no more than *thought forms*, creatures created out of the intense desires, dreams and aspirations of individuals still very much alive in the corporeal world.

THE ELDERS AND GLOBAL DISASTER

Once I accepted the fact that the Elders are a group who work very closely to the Angelic Kingdom, I was then allowed to work with them and be privy to some of their most secret teachings. Although they appear to me monastically attired, I have learned that they are beings of light from an advanced race that once inhabited the earth long before life as we know it existed here. A global disaster forced them to vacate the earth and take up residency on another planet, in a far off universe. They informed me that although they are from the far off past, they are also from the distant future, giving a whole new meaning to the phrase, *'BACK TO THE FUTURE'*.

As well as being an extremely effective method of establishing a relationship with angels, the Angels' Book of Promises is also a therapeutic exercise and a spiritual process that encourages in the user the development of a much deeper awareness and knowledge of Angelic Beings and the universe. Although use of the book is fairly straightforward, the connection it establishes with the universe precipitates spiritual consciousness and helps with the release of a much deeper, subjective knowledge that you never knew you possessed.

CHAPTER FOURTEEN

CHAKRAS, ANGELS
AND THE INDIGO CHILD

For thousands of years, long before the development of western science, Eastern esoteric traditions have taught that the human organism is composed of seven bodies, and that each one is constructed of a much finer material than the one below it. The fundamental principles of Eastern philosophy further state that there is a connecting force that binds each body to the other, and that the energy created by this force culminates into coruscating cosmic whirlpools, called 'Chakras'. Although it is taught that there are hundreds of minor chakras strategically located all over the subtle anatomy, there are in fact seven major chakras which are considered primary. These are situated across the surface of the 'etheric' body in the spinal tract. Chakras which literally mean 'wheels' or 'circles' in ancient Sanskrit, are connected to the endocrine glands and nerve plexuses through an extensive system of channels called nadis, along which flows energy (prana) from the chakras to the organs of the physical body, in the endless process of maintaining balance in body, mind and spirit. Although all seven major chakras are there potentially at birth, only one actually functions for the first 12 months of the life of the baby. This is located at the base of the spine and is called in Sanskrit Muladhara. This chakra is believed to be responsible for the instinctive actions of the child's existence until it reaches its second year, at which point the second chakra, Svadisthana becomes active. The third chakra, Manipura, becomes active when the child is three years old, and in its fourth year, Anahata, the heart centre becomes active. Combined with Sahasrara, the seventh chakra on the crown of the head, a connection with the

Celestial Light is formed. The heart centre is responsible for sensitivity and feeling, and with the support of the crown chakra, which is responsible for Cosmic Consciousness, the child's soul is polarised, thus maintaining its connection with the angels presiding over it. The fifth and sixth chakras, Vishudda and Ajna, together form a bridge of consciousness allowing the child to have a transcendental experience with angels. By the time the child reaches the age of seven all seven major chakras are fully active, ensuring that the child's consciousness is focused fully on its new environment. In fact, the chakras are like small lotus flowers whose petals increase as they ascend the spine; one of the reasons why spiritual consciousness is symbolically represented in eastern tradition by the lotus flower. Some schools of thought believe that chakras are like cosmic banks and contain all experience from previous incarnations. As the child's consciousness increases, so this experience is slowly released enabling the young individual's awareness and intelligence to fully develop.

INDIGO CHILDREN AND ANGELS

Occasionally a child is born into this world with all seven chakras fully vivified into coruscating whirlpools of colour and vitality. From a very early age such children exhibit remarkable skills far beyond their years, and are today referred to as *Indigo Children*. The exceptional abilities of the Indigo Child have totally baffled scientists and psychologists, many of whom have been forced to pose the questions 'Who are these children? Where do they come from?'

The skills exhibited by the majority of Indigo Children nearly always occur long before they are old enough to attend school and even without pre-school tuition or so called parental 'hot-housing'. One example is that of a severely handicapped 14 year old boy who had been born profoundly deaf, dumb and blind, and who had also sustained some degree of brain damage at birth. His future looked quite grim and all that his mother and father could do was care for him. However, one morning his parents were astounded when they went into the lounge to investigate who was playing such beautiful music on the grand piano they had recently purchased. They watched in amazement as their son's fingers moved gracefully across the keys, and sounding to all intense and purposes like a professional concert pianist, even though neither his mother nor father could play the piano at all.

One other example is of a severely disabled boy who was also profoundly deaf and dumb who amazed his parents with his incredible artistry with oil paints they had bought him for Christmas. They stood watching him dumfounded as he held a brush between his toes and one in his hand and began painting two beautiful simultaneous landscapes, both of which were in the style of old masters. There are innumerable examples of so-called Indigo Children all over the world, some say an indication that the human race as a whole is now going through an amazing spiritual epoch, bringing us closer to the Angelic Kingdom of Light.

THE BROW CHAKRA - AJNA

This very important chakra, located between the brows, in the seat of the traditional *Third Eye* is traditionally coloured Indigo and is responsible for the ability to actually 'see' clearly. Although this chakra is fully developed in those who are mediumistically inclined, the brow chakra of Indigo Children is extremely powerful and is totally focused on the supersensual side of the universe. This would suggest that Indigo Children are always in touch with angels and the Celestial Light. Some Indigo Children may even be a manifestation of reincarnated angels born in this life primarily as an example what is to come and to encourage the rest of humanity towards the Celestial Light.

As we evolve in Spiritual consciousness we begin to have an

abiding sense of the reality of the existence of the Supreme Power; and as our awareness of this develops we find that sense of human brotherhood, of human relationship gradually coming into consciousness. It is clear that we neither get these transcendental feelings from our instinctive mind nor do we experience them at an intellectual level; our spiritual mind does not function contrary to the intellect, but quite simply transcends the intellect. In fact, it passes down to the intellect certain truths that it finds in its own region of the mind, and the intellect reasons about them. But spiritual knowledge does not originate with intellect. Intellect is cold; Spiritual Mind is warm and alive with transcendentally high feelings. In more ways than we know are we being influenced by Angelic Beings whose sole intention is to bring the human race to a state of understanding and awareness of them and the Celestial Light.

SPECIAL PEOPLE

Apart from Indigo Children, there are people in whom an angel can be seen. Although we frequently use the term 'angel' to describe someone with a kind and benevolent nature, there have been individuals throughout antiquity who stand out from others, by their deeds, their kindness and their actions. It has been suggested that such people are also the manifestations of reincarnated angels.

CHAPTER FIFTEEN

ANGELS WHO LIVED AS PEOPLE

From as far back as I can remember I have prayed, more as a discipline and show of gratitude for the help I have received over the years rather than an act of worship. Every evening at ten precisely, I would retreat to my bedroom to pray and to spend fifteen minutes in meditation. I have always believed in actually falling to my knees to pray, just as a child would do each night before climbing into bed. I remember many years ago after I had gone through recovery and was more or less convalescing at my mother's home. It was the beginning of December and my room was in total darkness. I had finished praying and remained on my knees for a few moments longer imbibing the overwhelming silence, when an extremely intense bright light shone inside my head. Although it was the strangest experience I have ever had it was very calming and filled me with a sense of peace and serenity. The light remained inside my head for approximately ten minutes before gradually fading leaving me once again in total darkness. I experienced the unusual phenomenon several times after that, and on each occasion I was filled with a sense that I had been touched by an angel. There is no other way to describe the very surreal and transcendental experience. Although today it does not happen as frequently as it did then, I do still occasionally experience it, particularly when I am seeking an answer to a problem, or perhaps feeling a little down or under the weather. However, it was some time later that I found out exactly what the light inside my head actually meant. I began sitting in a development circle to refine and fully under-stand the abilities that had been with me since I was a child, under the supervision of Sylvia Alexio, an elderly and much respected medium who had been educated in a Rudolf Steiner school, and was one of the most spiritual people I have ever known in my life. It was she who explained to me that the unusual light inside my head was a clear indication that the celestial beings who had been watching over me were close and endeavouring once again to make their presence felt. It all made sense to me, and from then on I had no doubt whatsoever what I wanted to do with my life and that as always I was living beneath the wings of angels.

In my opinion, if Miss Alexio, (as she was fondly known,) was not herself an incarnation of an angel, she was most certainly one of the many unique individuals who are greatly influenced by the Kingdom of Angels. It is quite easy to embellish a story until it becomes something it is not, but everyone who knew Miss Alexio were truly humbled in her presence. She lived a simple life in a one room bedsit in a fairly nice area of Liverpool. She was a very much loved lady within the confines of the Spiritualist movement, and knowing that she had no surviving family everyone would give her presents at Christmas time. In fact, even those who scarcely knew Miss Alexio would make sure that they bought her a little gift at Christmas, and she always showed her appreciation by giving them a short spiritual message. Miss Alexio's one and only vice was an occasional cigarette, and ironically it was that which sadly caused her death. She had apparently been smoking in bed when the duvet somehow caught fire. Although she was rescued, her burns were so extensive that she lived only five days after. I visited her every day in hospital – along with many others – and on the day before she died I was standing by her bed watching her unrecognisable face as she tossed and turned in a semi-comatose state. She suddenly turned to face me and muttered in a low voice, 'tell your tall friend to come into the room.' As I was the only one there, I thought perhaps someone else had come to see her. I turned round to see Tall Pine, my spiritual mentor, standing in the doorway behind me, his arms folded across his chest and his dark eyes fixed on Miss Alexio. Although she was barely conscious she had seen him. A gentle smile broke across her lips and she lapsed into a deep sleep. Sadly, Sylvia Alexio passed away the following morning. One of Miss Alexio's close friends, the president of one of the Spiritualist churches she served as a medium, phoned me a few days later. She explained that she was the executor of Miss Alexio's will, and she had been clearing what was left of her belongs from the flat. The wardrobe and cupboards were full of unopened Christmas presents, a huge collection of gifts she had received from friends over the years. Miss Alexio's needs were few, and although she appreciated all the attention, she had very little need for the many gifts she had been given. She still comes to see me whenever I need a helping hand, and her visits are always preceded with the sweet fragrance of her familiar perfume.

TERESA HELENA HIGGINSON

Most saints and angelic individuals are always so far removed in time, that what we know of them is mostly anecdotal. Nonetheless, our faith is sufficient to make them come alive in our consciousness, thus perpetuating their name forever in time. However, there is one lesser known modern day angel whose spiritual life caused her great pain and hardship. Teresa Helena Higginson was a 19th century prophet, seer and marked with wounds of the crucifixion. This diminutive and very humble lady, was born in 1844, and was destined for a very unusual spiritual life. In 1854, at the age of 10, she was sent with her sisters to be educated in the Convent of Mercy in Nottingham, England, where she stayed until she was 21. She then went to live in St Helens, Merseyside, with her family, where they remained for a while until her father's business got into financial difficulties, and as a result he was made bankrupt. Circumstances then forced the Higginson family to move to Liverpool, where Teresa used her sewing skills to make extra money to make ends meet. The family then moved to Egremont, Wirral, but here Teresa was too ill to work and remained in bed at home, where her sisters nursed her back to health. When she had sufficiently recovered, Teresa eventually got a job as a teacher, and very quickly won the hearts of everyone. She was extremely religious and was known to devote two hours each day to prayer. She began to have prophetic visions and sought guidance from a Catholic priest by the name of Father Powell, who became her confidant and spiritual advisor. He was initially concerned for her psychological health, but eventually became convinced that Teresa's visions were genuine. Teresa also confided in her friend, fellow teacher, Susan Ryland, that she was frequently visited by Our Lady. As a mark of respect for the Holy visitation she would sometimes fast for days and spend up to two hours in prayer and meditation. She and Susan took rooms together, and her friend frequently witnessed Teresa in a trance-like state, with blood oozing from wounds in her hands and feet. Father Powell witnessed Teresa in states of 'ecstasy' and speaking in a voice that was not her own.

THE DEVIL

A disembodied hand would sometimes be seen throwing furniture about the room whilst she was asleep, and her friend Susan Ryland, would occasionally witness an unseen force pulling her violently from the bed. Teresa told Father Powell that it was the devil and that she frequently had to fight for her life. All attempts to exorcise the demon failed, and so her torment relentlessly continued.

PROPHECIES OF FUTURE EVENTS

Teresa Helena Higginson's unusual abilities ranged from writing copious amounts of script in handwriting completely different from her own, to levitating some feet from the floor, as well as prophesying future events. She prophesied that huge flying machines would attack Britain in a great war, and that long ships would sail beneath the waters of the seas. Her unusual life caught the interest of Pope Pius X who granted her an audience. It is well documented that Teresa had a profound effect upon him, and it was said that he remarked that she was a special child of God. Although Teresa Higginson's prophesies were well documented there were many people who were sceptical and accused her of being a false prophet. Nonetheless, her friend and confidant, Father Powell and other loyal devotees were relentless in their support. Father Powel witnessed all of Teresa's extraordinary phenomena, and always made certain to keep a record of what had occurred should ever he need to speak up against her critics. Teresa Helena Higginson taught in schools all over the UK, and in 1905, whilst preparing to return to her family home in the little village of Neston, Wirral for Christmas, she suffered a stroke and died. Her body was brought back to Neston, where her grave can be found today in the graveyard of St Winefrides, little Neston, where it is visited by hundreds of people each year. The simple stone cross is adorned with all sorts of religious artefacts and flowers, left by those who seek a blessing from the little Angel who is buried there. Steps are now being taken to beatify Teresa Helena Higginson who has become known as the 'Contemplative Saint.'

Many people proclaim that Teresa Helena Higginson was an angel incarnate and that she chose to live the celibate life she did out of sheer compassion. If Teresa was not an angel, just like Miss Sylvia Alexio, she was most definitely influenced by the Kingdom of angels.

JOAN OF ARC
Another example of an individual who was greatly influenced by angels was Joan of Arc, (1412 – 1431), probably the best known

canonised, historical figure of all time. She claimed to have been visited by the Archangel Michael on numerous occasions, and was instructed by him to lead her country into war. Saint Joan stuck by her story to the end, and at the age of nineteen was martyred for her beliefs. Had she not been visited by the apparition of Archangel Michael, she may never have secured such an exalted position in religious and secular history. Her first encounter with Archangel Michael took place when she was just thirteen and gathering rosemary and lavender in her father's garden on a warm summer's day. The euphonic sounds of the bells of the nearby chapel began to ring, piercing the warm summer air and making the whole ambience of the beautiful day even more perfect. It really all began when she distinguished a voice intermingled with the sound of the melodic tones of the bells. The voice gave her clear instructions pertaining to the future of her country. In fact, Joan claimed that it was from then on that the Archangel Michael visited her bathed in a beautiful golden light, and that each time he called he was accompanied by other angelic figures. He told her that she was to take up arms against the English, and that she would also be visited by saints Catharine and Margaret from whom she should seek counsel. Saint Joan was branded a heretic and accused of being insane. Her accusers said that if Archangel Michael was really guiding her, why did he not save her from the horrific ordeal of being burned at the stake? Perhaps martyrdom was an integral part of the plan, and Joan knew this from the very beginning of her visitations. Joan was obviously an instrument of an omnipotent power, and many have proclaimed her as 'Heaven's Angel here on Earth.'

SWEDENBORG VISITED BY ANGELS

Scientist, mathematician and inventor, Emanuel Swedenborg (1688-1772), claimed that his life was spiritually transformed when he was visited by angelic beings. In 1745, Swedenborg was visited by a spirit who allegedly informed him that he was being instructed by God to reveal the true nature of creation. Although Swedenborg was a highly educated man who had always held firm scientific views of life and death, he was totally convinced that his spirit visitor was a messenger of God – an angel from heaven. Whatever it was that appeared to Emanuel Swedenborg it definitely transformed his life from that of someone who had fixed views, to one who was able to look at life from a metaphysical and spiritual point of view. Swedenborg's visitations caused an incredible spiritual transformation in him to occur, so much so that he devoted the best part of his life writing voluminous theological treatises, two of which were *Heaven and Hell* and *Arcana Ceolestias*.

Swedenborg's very first angelic encounter transpired on a vacation in London. He was in an elegant English Inn, resting in an armchair and warming his hands in front of the fire, only vaguely aware of the other guests chatting. Although in the middle of the day, he suddenly became aware that a silence had descended, the fire had almost died and the room was in veritable darkness. Thinking that he had probably fallen asleep, he retrieved his watch from his vest pocket and checked the time. His suspicions had been confirmed – only a few minutes had elapsed and he had not fallen asleep. Swedenborg's attention was drawn to a figure of a young handsome man standing behind him. The figure was radiant and splendidly dressed. Somewhat confused, Swedenborg looked around the room for signs of the other guests. However, not only was the room empty, but there was also the noticeable absence of furniture. In fact, to all intents and purposes, he might well have been somewhere else. The angelic apparition addressed him as Emanuel, and explained that he was an angel who had come to teach him about the true purpose of life, further explaining that he knew that Swedenborg had tired of his materialistic ways, and knew that he wanted far more. 'You are needed to act as a modern-day prophet, and to carry on the tradition begun by the ancient prophets of the Bible.' The angel's words were clear and were the beginning of Swedenborg's spiritual metamorphosis.

WESTERN CONCEPTION OF ANGELS

In contemporary Western culture, angels are depicted as perfect beings with powerful white wings. Although these archetypal, romanticised images of angels popularised by European artists became increasingly more fashionable after the renaissance, it is easy now to fully understand why this was the case. There was and still is a great need for us to have ethereal beings with supernatural powers to look up to for help in times of great need. Angels fit all the criteria, which is probably the reason why they are integral parts of the religious doctrines of Judaism, Christianity and Islam. Because of the experiences I have personally had with angels, I have never doubted their existence for one moment. Besides, if they did not exist I am quite certain that our need for them alone would cause them to evolve somewhere deep within our souls.

CHAPTER SIXTEEN

NOT ALL ANGELS HAVE WINGS

It may sound ridiculous to a person who does not particularly have a fondness for animals, but occasionally a dog or cat may come into your life that is so special as to make you wonder where on earth it came from. I'm not just talking about a gentle loving pet, but a creature that appears almost like a human in the wrong body and is remarkable in every way. A loving dog or cat touches its owner's heart in a way that no human can, and quite often they come into our lives at just the right time, perhaps when you're grieving for the loss of a loved one, or even another pet. Nobody really knows what it is about animals, but they most certainly do possess something quite special that is very often not of this world. I must confess that I am speaking as an animal lover, and so I suppose to a sceptic or non-animal lover I am quite bias. Nonetheless, too many things connected to animals have happened to me during my life to be dismissed as mere chance or coincidence. Take the ghostly apparition of a dog bathed in a golden light that led four very young and frightened soldiers through the dark smoke-filled trenches in France during the First World War. Their battalion of Welsh Fusiliers had been under attack for most of the night, and the only ones to survive the terrifying ordeal were Ken Farsley and his three friends. The four young soldiers struggled desperately to negotiate their way through the smoke-filled maze of trenches, strewn with mutilated bodies and debris making their route almost impossible. When it seemed that all was lost, Ken Farsley's attention was suddenly caught by a dog surrounded by a bright light, barking at them, from a distance of no more than five meters away and obviously wanting them to follow it. Although they thought the ghostly apparition was simply the effects of gas inhalation, they knew they had nothing to lose. The four soldiers scrambled their way over the debris and followed the dog through the blackness of the thick smoke, not stopping until it had led them to the safety of another battalion of the Welsh Fusiliers in a trench only approximately forty meters away. Even though safety unbeknown to the young soldiers was only a short distance away, it would have been impossible for them to find their way through the maze of smoke-filled trenches. Ken Farsley and his friends could not believe it, and when they looked for their canine rescuer it was nowhere to be seen.

Ken Farsley told me this story before he died in 1995 at the age of eighty four, and it was as fresh and clear in his mind then as if it had happened a week before. He told me that from a child he had always believed in Angels, and in the trenches he had prayed to his own guardian angel for help. Was Ken Farsley an animal lover? 'No!' he told me. But he became one after that incident.

INFLUENCED BY ANGELS

This is just one of hundreds of stories about ghostly animals coming to the rescue of humans. Even if you dismiss the suggestion that the ghostly dog was an angel coming in answer to Ken Farsley's prayer, one cannot ignore the fact that the dog was most certainly not of this world. It is known that there are some angels who preside of the animal kingdom and influence them to come to the rescue of those in need. Why else would the ghostly dog choose to help the young soldiers by guiding them to safety?

Strange though it may sound, many people are offended by the very suggestion that animals have souls, let alone that Angels can manifest as a dog or cat. Nonetheless, there is far too much evidence to support this, and over the years hundreds of people – both animal lovers, and non-animal lovers – have related their stories to me.

GUIDE DOG RETURNS AS AN ANGEL

There was the story of the visually handicapped woman who was devastated by the sudden death of her faithful guide dog at the age of 18. Bess was not only Mary Griffith's constant companion, but she was also her best friend, and even slept in Mary's bedroom with her. It was only when Mary accepted the fact that she could not live a normal life without a dog to guide her that she agreed to take a newly trained Labrador purely on a trial basis. After only a week Mary protested that the new dog could not in any way take the place of her faithful Bess. The young Labrador's actions appeared clumsy and would occasionally lead Mary across a busy main road when it was not clear. The Guide Dog Society responded to Mary's protestations and came to see her. Mary was distraught and was adamant that the dog was not suitable. 'It may well just be that the new dog is picking up feelings from you and making it nervous?' Mary reluctantly accepted the woman's explanation and agreed to give it another couple of weeks.

Over the following few days Mary made every effort to relax with the new dog and this seemed to work. The new dog behaved with a more confident manner and did everything exactly as it was trained to do. Several trips to the High Street were successful and Mary had to admit that she now felt more relaxed and confident being guided by the new dog.

Mary agreed to accept the new dog and immediately named her Chloe. It wasn't until the vicar called unexpectedly to see Mary that she realised exactly what had happened. 'I see you've got a friend for Bess?' he smiled and sipped his tea. 'Even though she's getting on a bit she's training the new dog well!'

'What do you mean?' Mary was puzzled. 'Bess...'

Before Mary could finish the vicar quickly interjected, 'I was coming out of the Post Office yesterday and I saw you walking down the High Street. Bess seemed to be guiding her new companion and checking that she did everything correctly.'

Mary was speechless, and just smiled thoughtfully as a tear trickled down her face, and her faithful dog's name fell almost soundlessly from her lips, 'Bess, my sweet Bess....'

Mary Griffiths was a neighbour of my mothers, and was and still is practical and down-to-earth. She was not someone who would exaggerate or make up stories, particularly those involving her beloved dog Bess.

Some would say that this story is just an example of how our pets can reach out to help us from beyond the grave, whilst I would say this is a good example of why *Not All Angels Have Wings*.

AN ANGEL CALLED ROSE

As I have already said, from the age of two up until I was fifteen years old I spent most of my life in Mary 2 Ward, Alder Hey Children's Hospital in Liverpool, England. I was never in any longer than eight weeks at a time, and once all the exploratory tests had been done I would then be discharged. This was the 1950s when I suppose hospitals were still very Victorian in style, particularly in England, in comparison to hospitals today that is. I suppose one could say that Mary 2 Ward became my second home, and I always had the same bed each time I was admitted, by the window overlooking the park, and was always looked after by the same nurses. Once the first couple of days were over, to be honest, I quite enjoyed being in hospital, even if it did mean being away from my family. Hospital is nearly always a daunting experience to children at the best of time, and when facing the unknown it can be terrifying. I was quite used to seeing things nobody else could see, and I very often saw ghostly forms in old fashioned clothes walking around the ward in the middle of the night. In England in the 1950s they did not have the advantage of dimmer switches on the lighting; at 9 o'clock every night the Night Nurse would place a black cloth over each light, an indication to all the children in the ward that night had come and it was time to sleep. I hated the night time as this meant I was forced to watch my ghostly visitors – nurses and doctors long since dead, carrying on their duties from another world. Even tightly closing my eyes failed to shut them out of my head, and although they meant me no harm, their activities persisted until I had fallen asleep.

It was 1953 and approximately eight weeks before Christmas. I was seven years old and had calculated that I would be discharged the day before Christmas Eve. This meant that I would still be in hospital when the Liverpool Football team visited each ward, each one dressed as Santa Claus and laden with presents for the children. For me this was the most exciting part of being in hospital. The Christmas tree and decorations were already up in the ward and I was reading a comic and waiting for afternoon tea to be served, when two hospital porters came to collect me. Instead of taking me in a wheelchair for an X ray, as they usually did, this time they actually pushed my bed from the ward, into the elevator, and then pushed me to some remote part of the hospital I had never seen before. Without any explanation I was left in a deserted ward strewn with old screens and other pieces of discarded equipment, alone and terrified. Some of the windows in the ward were covered with black shutters, and the fading light of day filtered through the grime on the other windows casting eerie shadows across the wooden floor. I was petrified and wondered why I was there and what was going to happen to me. It was then that I encountered Nurse Rose, the elderly lady with a kind face and gentle voice. She was dressed in an unusual nurse's uniform and her face seemed to glow brightly. She told me her name was Nurse Rose and that she had been sent to look after me. I was somehow comforted by her presence and her gentle voice was reassuring. 'You'll be all right!' she told me, as she left the ward. I must have been there for over two hours when around twelve doctors walked into the ward with my consultant Dr McCandless. They all took turns examining me and asking me questions about the way I dealt with my illness, and then they left without so much as a goodbye. I was alone again and now the day had nearly gone. It was then that Nurse Rose returned to see if I was ok. She remained in the ward for some time, and I couldn't understand why she was busying herself in a ward that had obviously not been in use for a long time. I heard a noise coming from the elevator outside the ward and almost immediately Nurse Rose bade me farewell and hurried from the ward leaving me alone once again. The porters came in to collect me, and Jim the older one, stopped to pick something from the covers at the end of the bed. 'What's this?' he smiled. 'Has your girlfriend been to see you?' he gave me a mischievous grin as he handed me a single red rose. I knew immediately that Nurse Rose had left it for me. She was obviously an Angel – and most probably a nurse from days gone by. At one point Nurse Rose leaned over my bed to straighten the covers and secure them under the mattress and I could smell her unusually sweet fragrance. In fact, it lingered in the ward long after she had left. Although I was taken to the ward at least on one other occasion, I never saw Nurse Rose again. The reason for this may have been because the next time I was taken to the abandoned ward I wasn't left there quite as long. She was definitely not a living person, and was just one of many 'Angel' experiences I was to have during my childhood. Nurse Rose may not have been the archetypal idea of an angel with which we have grown up, but as I have previously said 'Not All Angels Have Wings'.

ACTING ON BEHALF OF ANGELS

It would be ridiculous to suggest that all those with a desire to help from 'beyond' the grave are angels. However, sometimes you are forced to question what you think you know and very often find yourself with a completely different conclusion. I frequently wonder how I would view the concept of angels had

I been born into a life free of sickness. Nonetheless, illness combined with my self-created hell has brought me to this point in my life and I do now look back with great appreciation and thanks.

During my recovery from the battering both my body and brain had sustained during my drug abuse years, I was frequently overcome by an immense darkness in which I decided to end my life. However, on each occasion an invisible hand was always proffered to lead me towards the safety of the light. This may sound very much like an Evangelical discourse on how to find God, but believe me as far as I am concerned there is no other way to describe how I have always been helped. On one particular cold and frosty day I decided that I could no longer go on causing my family anguish and distress, and decided to end it all. Although I had no idea how exactly I was going to do it, I just knew that I somehow I had to put an end to my painful and miserable life. I made my way to a Catholic Church a few streets away from my mother's house, where I often went to sit quietly for an hour or two whenever I was feeling depressed. As I made my way along the main road leading to the church, I seemed to be walking in slow motion, with everything passing by, almost as though I was in a dream. I remember looking through the open door of a vandalised empty house, and thinking to myself that it had been occupied only the day before; or at least, so it seemed to my depressed mind. I ascended the stone steps leading to the church door, and then made my way slowly down the aisle towards my usual place just in front of Saint Teresa of the Roses, where I sat with my head buried in my hands, my sobs echoing through the empty church. My attention was suddenly caught by a deep, and yet warm Irish voice. 'Hello, my son, can I help you?' I looked up to see a tall, grey haired middle-aged priest standing there smiling at me. Slightly embarrassed, I quickly brushed a tear from my cheek as he gestured for me to move along so that he could sit beside me. I felt as though I was in the company of an old friend, and just poured my heart out to him. I told him everything about my life from beginning to end. I really did expect a long religious lecture, but when I had finished he just pulled himself tiredly to his feet, made the sign of the cross, giving me his blessing, and then said, 'I am quite sure that your pain ended with the steps up to the church.' He turned and made his way down the aisle towards the door. I did not hear the door close, and so I turned to see where he had gone, but the church was completely empty. I did feel much better having spoken to the nice priest, and felt as though a great weight had been lifted from mind. I thought no more about the incident, until several weeks later I decided to return to the church to thank the middle-aged priest. I presumed that he lived in the house next door to the church and so I made my way up the pathway towards the front door. However, before my hand even reach the knocker a lady opened the door holding a duster in her hand. I explained that I had come to see the priest, but before another word was spoken a young man appeared behind her. 'Yes, can I help you?' he smiled politely. 'I'm Father McNamara.'

'No,' I stuttered almost apologetically, 'I'd like to see the other priest.' I naturally thought that I had made a mistake, and made my apologies before turning to make my way back down the pathway towards the street. Before I could reach the gate the woman called me. She disappeared inside the house and returned a few moments later holding a framed photograph. 'Is this the priest you wanted to see?' She held the photograph in front of me. I nodded excitedly, 'Yes, that's him. Unfortunately, I didn't get his name. I spoke to him in the church and I just wanted to thank him.'

The woman smiled thoughtfully, a look of sadness in her eyes. 'You'd have a job, young man. This is father Dewers. He died nearly ten years ago. He was a lovely man. You're not the first person to have spoken to him in the church – his church.' She raised her brows and smiled. 'Father Dewers was an angel – an angel in every sense of the word. He obviously took an interest in you. You are well blessed, my dear!'

My encounter with the priest was somehow much more meaningful than I had previously thought, and now I felt even more determined to live my life in the way I was meant to live it. Over the past years I had always felt that I was taking the long way home. Now I know exactly why!

CHAPTER SEVENTEEN

DREAMS AND THE FINAL ANALYSIS

I am surmising that you have read through this book from cover
to cover and have either decided to create your own Angels'
Book of Promises or have already done so. Whatever conclusions
you have reached, it is important to look upon your book as
being almost magical and possessing a power that can transform
your life both emotionally and spiritually. The Angels' Book of
Promises will become empowered through your faith and belief
that it WILL work, and in time will transform the way you think
as well as the way you perceive the outward world and the
universe beyond. The Angels' Book of Promises will encourage
the development of an inner knowledge and *knowing* and will
also help you to understand the Universe and the Law of
Attraction.

SECRET KNOWLEDGE

The tradition of a recondite knowledge can be found in every
literary recorded age; a knowledge that could only be passed on
to those who could prove their worthiness to receive it. This
knowledge was very generally known under the term of the
Mysteries and was primarily concerned with the deepest facts of
man's origin, his nature and connection with supersensual
worlds and beings, as well as of course with the natural laws of
the physical world. These supersensual worlds and beings were
a direct reference to the multidimensional invisible universe
and the Messengers who traversed between them and the earth,
bringing to the masters the most sacred knowledge. This
knowledge could never be written down and could only be
given by teacher to pupil, mouth to hear. Students of the

mysteries were subjected to the most arduous and rigorous tasks, thereby proving that they were spiritually and morally equipped to receive it and would not in any way abuse or misuse it. There were many aspirants who fell by the wayside and were turned away as a consequence. These either continued their studies in secret until such time that they would be allowed to resume their education in the Mystery Schools, or they immediately prostituted what knowledge they had already gleaned from their failed studies, to establish themselves as teachers in their own right. Once a student of the Mystery teachings had passed through the various degrees necessary, they would then be initiated into the final level, and thus be allowed to enter the 'Chamber of Divine Knowledge'. Once there they would be instructed in the deepest and most precious facts pertaining to the evolution of the soul; the universal laws and the nature of Man and the Messengers of God. With the passage of time the purveyors of the Mystery Teachings were condemned and driven underground by their persecutors. Seeing that the end of the Mystery Schools was drawing near, and wanting to ensure that the valuable teachings would not be lost forever, the surviving masters meticulously recorded all that they knew, taking great care to transpose the text into a more understandable core of teachings. These teachings were termed 'The Lesser Mysteries' and were and still are open to interpretation, according to the spiritual understanding of the aspirant. The Mystery teachings clearly indicated that beings from another dimension frequently visited the earth to help mortals in times of sadness and despair.

The angels frequently visit us in dreams; unusual and very lucid dreams, the content of which is very often symbolic and needs to be carefully deciphered. Angel dreams are not like ordinary dreams and only begin to occur once we express the desire for them to come into our lives and help us with a turbulent situation. There are times when they come into our dreams unbidden, perhaps to answer a question that has been bothering us, or even to reassure us of someone's well-being. Of course, it would be foolish to suggest that all unusual dreams are angel dreams. Dr Sigmund Freud's explanation for dreams is that they are the sleeping mental fulfilment of the unexpressed wishes or desires of the person dreaming. In addition to what may be termed 'normal' dreams, these are the dreams which are given a specific character by certain drugs. From earliest times there have been various theories as to what dreams are. According to a belief quite prevalent among some savage races, the soul or mind leaves the body and travels to the spirit world, meeting with angels and the souls of deceased ancestors. Another theory supported in the text of most ancient esoteric writings is primarily supernatural.

ANGELS OF SLEEP

According to ancient texts a dream is a communication from the other world. It further states that whilst in the realms of sleep a privileged few are allowed to sojourn with the angels who instruct and counsel the sleeper on matters pertaining to his or her life. When we have a problem we are wisely advised to 'sleep on it!' Only to find that upon waking the answer to our problem is the first thing to appear in our consciousness. Once a relationship with angels has been well and truly established, you can rest assured that *they* will infiltrate your dreams. As there are angels to help with our trials and tribulations of life in general, so are there angels to watch over us whilst we sleep. In Greek mythology the angels frequently spoke to heroes in their sleep, instructing them on the strategies of war. In the scriptural story of Joseph, the dreamer of dreams, it is clearly illustrated that he frequently spoke to angels in his sleep. Shaman priests frequently induced sleep by imbibing a herbal narcotic which allowed their spirit body to sojourn with the angels who would give them glimpses of future events. As I have said elsewhere,

Nostradamus also went through the same process of imbibing a herbal narcotic causing him to fall into a trance-like state, in which he would glean information about the future. Nostradamus's prophesies were always extremely cryptic, and were very much open to interpretation. This is very often typical of angel dreams, examples of which will be given later on.

PREPARING FOR ANGEL DREAMS

Once you have embarked upon the amazing journey towards developing a relationship with the Kingdom of Angels, and have truly acknowledged that 'they' are finally responding to the entries you have made in your Angels' Book of Promises, you can expect them to infiltrate your life in many different ways. Although I have already explained the nature of angel dreams, I would now like to make a detailed analysis of the symbology of dreams in relation to one of the significant ways in which angels may very well communicate with you. There are innumerable books on the interpretation of dreams, but knowing when a dream has some deeper, spiritual significance is quite different altogether. The one thing I would like to stress at this point is that you should not become too obsessed with the subject of angels. Apart from stating the obvious implications of obsession, such as the psychological and emotional, obsessing over angels defeats the whole object of the exercise, the primary aim of which is to enhance the spiritual quality of your life on all levels of consciousness. As far as I have always been concerned, angels are a fact of life! They exist whether or not you actually believe in them, simply because they are an integral part of your existence and are deeply encoded into your spiritual and psychological being. It has been said of God: 'If God did not exist we would have to invent him.' The same has been said many times of angels and the Celestial Beings of Light. As humans we are in great need of such divine beings to watch over and guide us through the turbulent and traumatic periods of our life. Anyway, if angelic beings do not exist, from where in our consciousness do they originate? From time immemorial Angels have been an integral part of most religious cultures – messengers of god, ambassadors of an omnipotent power. Although some people perceive angels as mythological creatures, they are nonetheless now encoded into our biological makeup and are an integral part of our belief in God. As I have previously stated, it is a psychological fact that not all dreams are prophetic or have deep spiritual significance. The majority of dreams are no more than the mind filtering through unwanted and unnecessary data. However, you don't have to be endowed with spiritual or psychic abilities to connect with Angelic Beings during sleep. On the contrary, some dreams are extremely symbolic, and although one of the many dream books available can be used to decipher the secret code of dreams, *Angel Dreams* require a more detailed analysis with a consideration of all the data that actually makes up the dream. *Angels' Dreams* are very lucid and extremely unusual in content. If you have ever woken up after having a vivid and very uplifting dream, overwhelmed with the disappointment that it was just a dream and no more, then you have most probably had an Angel Dream. These are much more apparent when you have already expressed an interest in Angels, and become more consistent the more you learn about Angels. Let us take as an example a dream about a wide expanse of water, such as an ocean or the sea. As with any dream all aspects of it need to be considered in the analysis before a correct interpretation can be made. Generally speaking, in an ordinary dream, water symbolises the emotions. Clear, calm water portends emotional security, love or happiness. Turbulent and rough water portends the contrary, upheaval, insecurity and a problematic relationship. However, the structure of an Angel Dream is something quite different. Not only does it feel different, but it is very often not like a dream at all. For one thing an Angel Dream is usually in vivid, clearly defined colours, and is surreal but nearly always seems familiar, almost as though you have been there before. In an Angel Dream whether the water is rough or calm makes no difference, and it may even appear in colours you would never see in water, such as yellow, orange or even red. In the case of water the colours are important and need to be considered in the analysis. In the dream, although the colour of the sky may complement the colour of the water, that too may be unusual. Waking up after having a symbolic Angel Dream, the dreamer is often left with an overwhelming peaceful feeling of having had a very special experience. In fact, a similar dream may occur with absolutely no angel relevance at all, and you will know immediately upon waking that it was just an ordinary dream. Although Angel Dreams are so varied, I have listed some examples in the following chapter to help you. These are the most common of Angel Dreams, but from these you should have a fairly good idea how to decipher the symbology. Remember, the type of symbolism in the following examples usually only occur when there has been a deep interest expressed in angels. Once you have acknowledged their existence in your life, it is as though a trigger in your brain precipitates some subtle dream mechanism, encouraging your dreams to be more realistically meaningful.

CARING FOR YOUR ANGELS' BOOK OF PROMISES

I cannot stress too much the importance of taking great care of your Angels' Book of Promises. It must be treated as you would a sacred artefact, with reverence and great respect. Your treatment of it is what will make it special and magical. Initially you may look upon it as just a book, but once you have seriously begun to use it you should then see it as something quite special. When you are not using your Angels' Book of Promises keep it wrapped in black silk or velvet and placed out of sight of other people, securely in a drawer or even in a box that you can place in a cupboard well out of the reach of children.

WRITING IN YOUR BOOK

Although this has already been covered in an earlier chapter, the importance of making entries in your book needs to be reiterated once again. Never rush your entries and always take care to write neatly. Don't worry too much if your hand writing is not legible at the best of times, as your intention when writing is what really matters.

If you are not fortunate enough to obtain a book that is nicely decorated, then take your time in painting the cover colourfully with intricate patterns. Although your book should ideally have a hard cover, if you feel attracted to one that does not have a hardcover then use that. A hardcover ensures it longevity and is obviously more durable than one that is not.

Write *REQUEST* clearly on the left hand page, preferably in colour, perhaps green, and on the right hand page write *PROMISE* perhaps in the colour blue. Write your entries in a different colour to the headings and always make them stand out in some way. In other words, make the book your own, and even create a symbol for the cover that somehow represents you.

Although the very back of the book may be used to enter the names of people who are unwell, it would be much better to create a second book specifically for this purpose. In fact, your Angels' Healing Book. If you do this you must treat it in exactly the same way as your Angels' Book of Promises.

Although the book can be used without any of the rituals, meditations or scrying techniques shown in the previous chapters, it really does help with whole process and really makes the book sacred and special. Apart from all that the book must be dedicated before use (not every time) and also empowered by sitting quietly with it on your lap.

WHAT TO DO WHEN YOUR ANGELS' BOOK IS FULL

Although some people do like to keep their Angels' Book of Promises when it is full, primarily for sentimental reasons;

before beginning a new book the full one should ideally be ceremoniously burned. This fully discharges the book's energies in preparation for the creation of a new one. Should you follow this advice, never throw the full book on the fire in your home, but take it into the garden and burn it beneath some dry twigs or straw, followed by the words *'Now that its work has been fulfilled I offer this book to you.'* Even when your Angels' Book of Promises is full and you are ready to burn it, maintain the whole sacredness of it and assign it to the flames still unseen and untouched by anyone else. The burning of your book is an integral part of the whole ritualistic process, and so it is therefore important that you do not look upon the burning as destroying it simply because you no longer need it; but see it as an offering to the angels now that its work has been completed. If you decide to keep your full Angels' Book of Promises as opposed to burning it, then you must always keep it wrapped and locked away, and once you have created and begun to use a new book, the old one must never be taken from its covering even out of curiosity.

SYNCHRONISING WITH YOUR BOOK

Even when you are not using your Angels' Book of Promises, whenever you get a spare ten minutes sit quietly with it in your hands. This initially really helps with its empowerment and encourages it synchronicity with your own energies.

Last of all, all ways be mindful of why you have created the book and to whom it is dedicated. The Angels' Book of promises transcends prayer and is your own personal way of establishing a relationship with the angels watching over you.

CHAPTER EIGHTEEN

DREAM EXAMPLES

The Angel dream examples given in this chapter are only to give you some idea of their meaning. The onus is on the dreamer to work out the final interpretation of his or her dreams by meticulously keeping a nightly record of them. Keep a note pad and pen by the bedside, and try to wake yourself up as soon as the dream is over. It's no use tiredly trying to convince yourself that you will remember the dream in the morning, because more often than not the dream will have completely vanished from your mind as soon as you wake up. Occasionally Angel dreams are so vivid that you may well recall every detail with great ease. However, in the majority of cases the dream won't be remembered, so it is best to write down all the details of the dream as soon as you wake up.

A - DREAM
To dream of an angel or angels talking to you and then carrying you high above the clouds.

MEANING
Contrary to the obvious interpretation, this dream does not signify death and being carried to heaven. It is a dream that portends happiness and enlightenment, and indicates quite clearly that your aspirations towards making contact with Angels have been successful. This is usually a reoccurring dream.

B - DREAM
Banqueting at a table of plenty with people dressed in monastic robes you do not know.

MEANING

This is an extremely fortunate dream and portends availing opportunities and success in business or any other ventures. It is also an indication that you are going to make new and valued friends who hold great power.

B - DREAM

You dream of meeting a blind beggar.

MEANING

This dream warns you to change your ways and to be more honest with others. If the dream involves a beggar who is not blind, you are being told to be more compassionate and more generous to others.

C - DREAM

You dream that you have no electricity and are working in the light of many candles.

MEANING

This is a contemplative dream, which also contains a warning not to be too hasty. Generally speaking, the candles symbolise light and guidance from the angels.

C - DREAM

You dream that you are floating high above and through clouds and are surrounded by the blue of the sky.

MEANING

This dream does not signify that you have or are going to die; quite the contrary, this is a dream of spiritual upliftment and portends divine intervention and wisdom. The blue signifies that you may also be in need of healing.

D - DREAM

In the dream you see yourself as being dead and you are trying to attract the attention of your loved ones and friends but nobody can see you.

MEANING

The Angel interpretation of this dream is completely the opposite. This dream is telling you that you really lack confidence, and subconsciously would rather walk into a crowded room unnoticed. You are being told that you are quite special and receiving encouragement that you are not listening to.

D - DREAM

You dream that you are living in a world of perpetual darkness, and you are struggling to negotiate your way through it.

MEANING

With this dream the angels guiding you are telling you to listen more to that inner voice and allow them to show you the way. FAITH is the key word in this dream and you most probably lack faith in the angels supervising your life.

E - THE DREAM

An eagle or some other exotic bird holding a conversation with you, either audibly or telepathically.

MEANING

This dream portends financial difficulties coming to an end, and is a very lucky dream. In accordance with Shamanic tradition the bird is an angel in disguise and is the bearer of good news. It also symbolises wisdom being bestowed upon you and all your spiritual endeavours coming to fruition.

E - DREAM

You dream that you have a chicken that lays golden eggs, but no matter how hard you try, it will only produce one egg.

MEANING

This dream is warning you against lack of respect, greed and telling you to show gratitude. Take care, otherwise you might just lose all that you think you have gained.

F - DREAM

You see yourself flying over a beautiful terrain of luscious green meadows, hills and valleys. The dream is so real you can feel the wind in your face and smell the sweet fragrances of the season.

MEANING

Although being able to fly in a dream is quite common, a vivid dream of flying over a beautiful terrain is a typical Angel Dream, and is indicative of the Angels elevating you over your problems and transporting you to a place of safety, for example a more serene and peaceful life. Although the terrain appears beautiful and picturesque, in the dream you are being shown exactly how your life is going to be in the not-too-distant future. Pay particular attention to the colours in the dream; the brighter and more surreal the colours, the happier your life will be in the future.

F - DREAM

You dream that you possess incredible strength and power and amazing fighting abilities. You see yourself being attacked by a gang of thugs but fight them off with great precision, strength and ease.

MEANING

The Angel interpretation of this dream is simply that you will never falter or be let down. Although in the dream you see yourself fighting your assailants off with the expertise of a great fighter, you are being told that there is no need to be an expert fighter as your mind and wisdom will always protect you against adverse situations.

G - DREAM

In your dream you see or encounter God or god-like beings.

MEANING

This dream is self-explanatory and is more or less exactly what you dream. You are on the right path and you are being closely supervised during your spiritual development. You need to have faith in yourself and be more determined.

G - DREAM

You dream that you meet up with your spirit guide and he or she gives you instructions that you cannot remember upon waking.

MEANING

This is a dream of intuition and faith. You are being told to use your intuitive skills more and have more faith in those who are guiding you.

There is no need to hear what you are being told, your spirit guide will always work through your intuition.

H - DREAM

In your dream you are extremely happy even though in reality you are quite down and despondent.

MEANING

This dream is a sign of what is to come, and is telling you that happiness is purely a state of mind. Things are most certainly going to change for you, and so you are being warned to be patient.

H – DREAM

In the dream you see yourself walking across the mosaic floor of a grand hall, perhaps with a domed ceiling, and you hear your footsteps resound from wall to wall.

MEANING

Although generally speaking this dream can have many meanings, the Angel's interpretation is one of self analysis. The grand hall symbolises your mind and the yet undiscovered knowledge in it. One usually has this dream more than once. The dream is suggesting that you fill your mind with knowledge, perhaps by reading more and listening to others less.

I - DREAM

You dream of throwing a large pot of ink into a river and you watch as the dark substance forms patterns until the clear water is finally corrupted by the ink.

MEANING

Take great care not to interfere in the dreams and aspirations of someone close to you. Allow things to run their own course, and when something is complete do not try to make it more perfect.

I – DREAM

You dream that you are on an island and completely cut off from the mainland and the people you love.

MEANING

This is a fairly complicated dream and has been evolved in a complicated mind. You are being warned to be more open with your feelings, and to share your thoughts and feelings with those with whom you share your life. It is also a warning about praying for one thing and thinking another.

J - DREAM

You dream of a hangman's Jib, and although you can't see anyone you are overwhelmed with the feeling that you are about to be hanged.

MEANING

The meaning of this dream is completely the opposite. The Angel Dream interpretation is one of lack of responsibility. You need to now be responsible for your thoughts as well as your actions. Had you seen yourself actually being hanged, the dream would be telling you that you should not take too many chances with business or relationship ventures.

J - DREAM

You see yourself about to jump off a precipice into a rocky defile, but are saved by someone you do not know.

MEANING

You have an admirer and someone who desperately needs your friendship. This person's friendship would be good for you.

K - DREAM

You dream of killing someone you don't know, and see yourself hiding the body.

MEANING

This dream is telling you to get your affairs in order and not to be so dishonest with those who care for you. You are also probably putting important issues to one side

K - DREAM

You see yourself as a child flying a colourful kite.

MEANING

In the context of Angels this dream is quite significant. This is a dream of encouragement. The colours on the kite represent your spirituality, and the kite is indicative of your spirit being elevated. Seeing yourself as a child is telling you to have more faith – as a child would – and not to question things too much.

L - DREAM

You dream that you are travelling through the air towards an extremely bright light, and feel filled with anticipation and excitement.

MEANING

In the context of Angels this is a dream of great spiritual significance. It is not a journey towards the light of death – far from it! This is a dream of approaching opportunity and a breakthrough where the spirit is concerned, and indicates that you have made a 'connection' with your Guardian Angel or Angels.

L – DREAM

You dream that you are trying to get away from something, and you are limping and can't seem to move fast enough.

MEANING

In the context of Angels, this dream is warning you to slow down, perhaps even to face up to reality and your responsibilities.

M – DREAM

You dream that you are in the presence of the Virgin Mary or some other exalted lady.

MEANING

This dream is self-explanatory and represents Divine intervention in your life. Your prayers are being answered.

M - DREAM

You dream of either rolling around in mud, or simply trying desperately to wade your way through it.

MEANING

Strange though it may sound, in the context of Angels this dream is telling you to have a medical check-up, and is not symbolic of you having a difficult time.

N - DREAM

You dream that you are carrying a bag of nails that fall one by one through a big hole.

MEANING

Although quite a nonsensical dream, it is also quite complex. This dream is telling you to guard against false friends. In the context of Angels, nails symbolise security. You are most probably not secure in your relationships.

N - DREAM

You dream that you are standing in front of a man (or woman) who is smiling and nodding at you but you don't know why!

MEANING

Although this seems a silly dream, it is a dream of approval. Whatever you have done, or whatever you are planning on doing, the Angels who are guarding you totally approve.

O - DREAM

You dream that you are walking slowly through an olive grove and the sun is shining brightly.

MEANING

This is a very spiritual dream, and a dream in which all things need to be considered. The olive grove is quite significant and symbolises your deeper aspirations, your dreams and things you are endeavouring to achieve. The sun represents the spirit and the Divine power that is encouraging you in everything.

O - DREAM

You dream that you can hear a group of people chanting 'OM' over and over again.

MEANING

Although quite rare, this is an extremely unusual dream. It has great spiritual significance, and the word being chanted is the resonating sound of God, and a mantra that should tell you that you are definitely living your life in the presence of angels.

P - DREAM

You dream of an old man playing a pan's pipe or similar instrument.

MEANING

In the context of Angels this is also an extremely significant dream, and represents the need for harmony and peace in your life.

P - DREAM

You dream of Peace, and being in a peaceful, tranquil place.

MEANING

This dream suggests that your life is one of chaos, at least from a spiritual point of view. The need for peace is of great importance and should be sought at almost any cost.

Q - DREAM

You dream that you are on a very special quest but you're not quite sure what that is.

MEANING

This is a clear indication that your spirit is crying out for sustenance - for knowledge. You are being warned to pay more attention to the spiritual side of your life.

Q - DREAM

You dream that you are in the presence of a very beautiful queen who appears to be not of this world.

MEANING

This is a typical Angel Dream and one that is simply making it clear that you are being watched over and guided through your life, whatever your aspirations.

R - DREAM

In your dream you are running away from danger but you seem to be having difficulty moving your legs. This dream is different from the one mentioned previously where you are limping. In this dream everything usually looks grey and very bleak with absolutely no colour whatsoever.The mounting fear is overwhelming.

MEANING

The usual interpretation of this sort of dream greatly depends on your psychological state at the time, and usually indicates insecurities and worries. However, with an Angel Dream it is interpreted as not facing reality – and the Angels are preventing you from running away from your responsibilities, both material and spiritual.

R - DREAM

In your dream you are standing on the banks of a fast moving river and you need to get to the other side, but cannot.

MEANING

The interpretation is self-explanatory, and indicates that your emotional life is perhaps a little chaotic and needs to be sorted. Although you are being guided, you are in fact being told to make your own decisions.

S - DREAM

You dream that you are in a room full of silver; silver trophies, silver coins, medals and candlesticks. You see all manner of things made from silver.

MEANING

In the context of angels silver represents the sun – the universal spirit. This is an extremely lucky dream, portending success and personal development. However, the room represents your mind, and should this be dark and dismal, then the dream is telling you that you are too materialistic and wealth is all that you dream about.

S - DREAM

You dream that you are fending off many assailants with a huge broad sword, a fight that seems relentless and one you do not seem to be

winning.
MEANING
All things in this dream need to be considered. The sword symbolises your unrealised strength and power. You may not realise it but you are being well protected. The power and strength of the sword is your guardian angel, and the whole dream is an indication that you should have faith and be more determined.

T - DREAM
In your dream you are able to move objects with your mind, (telekinesis) and possess other amazing abilities, such as being able to levitate. But in the dream you feel as though you are someone else, perhaps not of this world.
MEANING
Although not an uncommon dream, the Angel interpretation is twofold: firstly, the dream is trying to make you aware of your full psychic/spiritual potential, and secondly, you are being told that you are in control of your own destiny and are about to break through into a new and exciting area of your life.
T - DREAM.
In your dream you see yourself speaking on the telephone but nobody is answering you.
MEANING
The telephone is the primary object of this dream, and is twofold in meaning. You need to work on your powers of communication, and also you are not receiving the answers to your questions. You need to change your approach to life and cultivate a new way of dealing with your problems and people around you.
T - DREAM
You are surrounded by many people chanting 'Truth, Truth, Truth,' to you.
MEANING
Although an unusual and extremely rare dream, it is a typical Angel Dream. This has a twofold meaning; one you are being challenged to

be truthful about your needs and intentions, and the other is calling
you to pursue Truth, regardless of the consequences.

U - DREAM

You dream that you are in a world where everything looks upside down
to you; even other people are upside down, No matter what you do you
cannot rectify the problem.

MEANING

This is quite a rare dream, but when it does occur you can rest assured
that you are blessed. In this dream the angels are telling you that you
are extremely gifted, and an unusual individual who appears to be the
odd one in your family. As a result of this you are probably made to feel
so uncomfortable that you are forever trying to change to be like
everyone else. You cannot change the way you are, and why should
you? Be yourself for the best is yet to come.

U - DREAM

You have a crazy dream that you are walking in the rain with your
open umbrella held down, and you are getting very wet!

MEANING

This dream is indicating that you are extremely careless. However, all
things in it need to be considered before a detailed analysis can be
made. Although you are careless, the umbrella is an available means of
protection for you. The rain also represents a cleansing ritual. So,
although you are careless, you are being looked after by the angels.

V - DREAM

You dream that either you are surrounded by violets, or you are
walking through a violet cloud that never seems to end.

MEANING

This dream is quite special, and is also a typical Angel Dream. Violet
is the highest colour in the spectrum and the colour of spiritual
consciousness and the crown chakra. Should you be involved in a
psychic development programme, this dream is giving you encour-
agement. Even if you are not, you are being overwhelmed with the

powerful healing rays of violet, and infused with its powerful spiritual vibrations.

V - DREAM

You have a nightmarish dream that you are in the company of vampires, who seem to be your friends.

MEANING

This is an angel's warning dream. Those who you think of as friends are only with you for either what you are or what you can give them. You must sort the wheat from the chaff, and get rid of those who are not genuine.

W - DREAM

You dream that it is a cold winter and you are having trouble walking into the wind that keeps pushing you back.

MEANING

This is a twofold dream: No matter how hard you work you do not seem to achieve very much. Just like the wind, circumstances always seem to push you back. Nonetheless, the wind tends to blow away all the dross and is fresh and clean. You may be struggling at the moment, but you can rest assured that there is something good on its way.

W - DREAM

You dream that you are throwing a coin into a wishing well and making a wish.

MEANING

This is a very fortunate dream and one that portends good luck, prosperity and happiness. The wishing well is a very good omen.

X - DREAM

You dream that you are playing a Xylophone before a large audience consisting of ethereal beings.

MEANING

This dream has a few meanings, all of which are good. Music in a dream symbolises harmony and happiness. Your ability in the dream represents coordination, dexterity and confidence. The audience repre-

sents the admiration you have from others. This dream portends success in all your endeavours, both material and spiritual.

X - DREAM

You dream that you have x ray vision and have the power to 'see' through people and even see what they are thinking.

MEANING

This is a good Angel Dream, and symbolises your latent spiritual abilities. You have more potential than you realise, and the angels are giving the encouragement you will never get from those with whom you share your life.

Y - DREAM

You dream that you are sailing in a yacht on calm waters. The sea and sky are clear blue, and the white mast is fully open against the wind as the yacht pushes its way through the clear water.

MEANING

The meaning of this dream is quite clear. The clear blue water and blue sky denotes spirituality and healing. Blue is a calming colour, stimulating and uplifting. You are being looked after by your guardian angel, and just as the yacht is being pushed by the wind through the water, so are you being encouraged all through your life.

Y - DREAM

You dream that you are in the company of a Yeti, that mysterious, hairy humanoid creature that lives in the Himalayas. It is friendly and protective towards you and you feel comfortable in its presence.

MEANING

This is an incredibly sacred and spiritual dream, and a typical Angel's dream. You have the potential to access a wealth of secret knowledge, and also possess unusual spiritual powers potentially. The strength and power of the Yeti is indicative of wisdom that is inherent within you. The angels are most certainly guiding and watching over you.

Z – DREAM

You dream that you are in an environment with zero temperature and *feel as though your whole body is gradually freezing up.*

MEANING

This is a warning dream. You lack emotion and do not appreciate the beauty of the world around you.

Z – DREAM

You dream that you are walking through a zoo but the animals there are completely unfamiliar to you.

MEANING

This is a typical angel dream and nothing whatsoever to do with animals. You have made a wrong decision where your business dealings are concerned and are now faced with dealing with a situation that requires you to be astute and cunning. You will overcome it in time.

These dreams are just a few examples I have selected from millions of different combinations and varieties of dreams. An ordinary dream book is of no use to you when interpreting Angel Dreams, as the source of these dreams lies in another place – perhaps even in another time. I have chosen these dreams and their meaning merely to give you an idea. However, the best interpretation is the one you yourself make upon waking. Always keep a pen and pad by your bed so you can keep a record of your dreams. Unlike ordinary dreams, Angel Dreams are a little easier to remember; nonetheless, you should still make a note of them as soon as you wake up.

The psychological as well as the spiritual implications of Angel Dreams cover a very broad spectrum of your life, unlike ordinary dreams which are associated with your psychological state at the time of dreaming. The ability to differentiate between an Angel Dream and an ordinary dream will come in time and with experience. However, initially you should be guided by your intuition.

You may also find that the stronger the affinity you develop with you Angels' Book of Promises, the more unusual your dreams will become. Even if you do not have actual encounters with angels, you can rest assured that they will be close to you by inspiring and influencing the decisions you make and the dreams you have. May your journey with angels always be fruitful.

FINAL ANALYSIS

To some the very idea of an Angels' Book of Promises would no doubt be dismissed as no more than a children's pastime and an extremely effective way of keeping children occupied. Although the Angels' Book of Promises is an extremely effective way of encouraging children to express their feelings, fears and wishes, it is also an ideal way of teaching them a moral and spiritual code and to encourage them to express their thoughts and feelings as opposed to keeping them in. Although the Angels' Book of Promises is ideal for children, it was written with adults in mind. The only prerequisite for its use is the strong belief that it will work. When used correctly I have found the Angels' Book of Promises to be an extremely powerful psychological/spiritual tool that can produce positive results very quickly. It seems to work on three very different levels. The psychological benefits are fairly obvious, inasmuch as the actual process of writing down the things that you need in the Angels' Book of Promises encourages the release of inner tensions and fears. As a psychological/spiritual tool it helps the writer to externalise his or her dreams and desires, thus impressing on the universe a blueprint of all those things he or she needs to be secure and happy. The spiritual implications are far-reaching and also help the writer to make a connection with those Angelic Ambassadors of Light who help and guide us through turbulent times. The Angels' Book of Promises also helps to promote self-harmony and is best described as a *Healing Balm for the Tired Mind.*

Working on the premise that we are the architects of our own destinies by the way we think, the Angels' Book of Promises encourages a much deeper and clearer understanding of the Great Law of Attraction simply through the extremely effective way it works.

As long as your Angels' Book of Promises is laid out in the

way I have explained and properly 'dedicated' to the angels in the way I have shown, it is not necessary to use all of the rituals and exercises given in the book. You may even choose to modify some of the exercises to suit you, or even create some new ones of your own; it really doesn't matter, as long as you do *believe* in the whole process and think about what you are actually writing in your book.

As I have explained previously in the book, I have used the Angels' Book of promises since I was a young boy and still continue to use it with some degree of success today. Angels are always near and are always ready and willing to come into our lives. However, you must always bear in mind that they will only bring into your life what they feel is necessary for your greater fulfilment and happiness. As long as your requests are not selfish or intended to harm others, and more importantly that you are prepared to do something in return for what the angels do for you, then your book will always work.

I wish you well in your use of your Angels' Book of Promises, and pray that like me you will always *Live your Life Beneath the Wings of Angels.*

Billy Roberts

6th Books investigates the paranormal, supernatural, explainable or unexplainable. Titles cover everything included within parapsychology: how to, lifestyles, beliefs, myths, theories and memoir.